60
second
solutions

SELLING

DAN RAMSEY

D&C
David and Charles

A DAVID & CHARLES BOOK
© F&W Media International, LTD 2011

David & Charles is an imprint of F&W Media
International, LTD
Brunel House, Forde Close, Newton Abbot, TQ12 4PU, UK

F&W Media International, LTD is a subsidiary of
F+W Media, Inc.
4700 East Galbraith Road, Cincinnati, OH 45236

First published in the UK in 2011

Text copyright © F+W Media Inc. 2011

The material in this book has been previously published
in *The Everything Sales Book*, published by Adams
Media, 2009.

F+W Media Inc. has asserted the right to be identified
as author of this work in accordance with the
Copyright, Designs and Patents Act, 1988.

A catalogue record for this book is available from the
British Library.

ISBN-13: 978-1-4463-0047-3 paperback
ISBN-10: 1-4463-0047-1 paperback

Printed in Finland by Bookwell for
F&W Media International LTD,
Brunel House, Forde Close, Newton Abbot, TQ12 4PU, UK

10 9 8 7 6 5 4 3 2 1

Senior Acquisitions Editor: Freya Dangerfield
Assistant Editor: Felicity Barr
Project Editor: Cheryl Brown
Proofreader: Freya Dangerfield
Art Editor: Sarah Underhill
Production Controller: Bev Richardson

F+W Media publish high quality books on a wide range
of subjects.
For more great book ideas visit: www.rubooks.co.uk

CONTENTS

Introduction   006

PART ONE: The principles of selling   010

PART TWO: It's all in the preparation   036

PART THREE: Getting a foot in the door   062

PART FOUR: The successful sale step by step   084

PART FIVE: The art of presentation   110

PART SIX: Follow up and follow through   134

Index   160

INTRODUCTION

Nothing happens until something is sold. Take a look around you. Someone has sold everything you see – from beans to buildings – to someone. Without sales, factories and stores would close worldwide, trucks would park, airplanes would be grounded, and virtually everyone would be unemployed. Fortunately, selling is alive and well. It contributes significantly to the economy, providing us with employment as well as something for us to spend our earnings on.

Unfortunately, the sales profession been damaged by an unscrupulous few who will say or do anything to win a sale. Happily, they are in the minority, and you can be reassured that selling is a satisfying and rewarding career that contributes to the lives of others. It doesn't have to be cutthroat, you don't have to be deceptive or greedy to be successful, and there are plenty of opportunities for those who sincerely care about their customers.

Wherever you are in your sales career – starting out or burning out – this book will give you guidance in fulfilling your aims.

the economy rolls forward on the wheels of sales

A COMMON SENSE GUIDE

60 Second Solutions Selling is written for people who are considering their first or twenty-first job in sales. It offers practical and proven advice gleaned from decades of experience and dozens of experts. It is a guide to selling in the real world.

Due to lack of good training, many retail salespeople get frustrated at the very start of their careers and quit, missing out on the opportunity to discover how rewarding a sales career can be. At the other end of the scale, experienced salespeople become disheartened, disappointed by yet another 'foolproof' selling method offered by a sales guru, which when tried, doesn't work for them.

You won't find any hypes, gimmicks, high-pressure tactics or unproven psychology here, just the simple guiding principle: help buyers make good choices. The solutions offered are all based on common sense. Wherever you are in your sales career, use them to build a better future for you, your employers and your customers. You'll learn how to find buyers, make successful presentations, solve customer problems, and keep them coming back time and time again. Most importantly, you'll feel good about being in one of the world's most valuable professions – sales.

everything you need to sell in the real world without selling your soul

FIND A SOLUTION

60 Second Solutions Selling offers 60 solid solutions
to improve your selling techniques and develop
your sales career. Each can be devoured in just one
minute, yet each will offer lasting inspiration to help you
achieve your career aspirations. The book is divided
into six parts, with ten solutions in each.

Part One starts by looking at what selling is all
about, explores what makes a good salesperson
and introduces some of the most powerful selling
techniques including the Golden Rule of Sales, sell
as you would want to be sold to. After all, selling isn't
rocket science; customers simply yearn for an honest,
trustworthy, helpful guide who can assist them in
making informed decisions.

*whatever the situation
you find yourself in, you'll
find a solution to seal
the deal*

Part Two prepares the groundwork,
and covers important topics as finding
customers and setting career goals. In
Part Three, the secrets of meeting with
prospective customers are revealed,
helping you to secure that all-important sales
appointment. Part Four walks you through the sales
meeting step by step to ensure you maximize your
chances of success. Part Five is about giving a
winning presentation, no matter what you are selling
and to whom. Finally Part Six looks at some of the more
challenging tasks you may face as your career
advances, including selling to multiple buyers and
writing a sales proposal for consideration. It also shows
you how to apply sales techniques to marketing yourself
so you can succeed in getting the best jobs in sales.

TOP TEN THINGS YOU'LL LEARN

1 Buyers purchase features and benefits, not products and services.

2 It is important to know your competition better than your buyers do.

3 Instead of selling on price, you must help your buyers understand the greater value of what you offer.

4 You can use suggestion and gentle persuasion to help your buyers make decisions.

5 Most buyers today have too many other choices than to be sold using fear and intimidation.

6 Buyers don't want you to be their best friend, they just want friendly assistance.

7 If your buyers trust you to be honest and accurate, they will buy more from you.

8 Buyers have a problem that you can solve; by asking relevant questions and listening to answers, you can help them buy.

9 Once you've earned a position of authority and trust, you can consult with your buyers to find the best solution to their problem.

10 Adding real or perceived value to transactions can improve your sales income.

part
one

part
one

THE PRINCIPLES
OF SELLING

01	What is selling?	012
02	Embrace your inner salesperson	014
03	Know what makes a good salesperson	016
04	The golden rule of sales	018
05	Understand the decision-making process	020
06	The art of persuasion	022
07	Help the buyer to make good choices	024
08	The power of the soft cell	026
09	Selling – the noble profession	028
10	Above all things, enjoy what you do	030

SOLUTION 1
WHAT IS SELLING?

The adage that nothing happens until a sale is made is true. Without a transaction (the exchange of goods, services, ideas, promises, or funds) the economy would come to a standstill.

To sell something is to inform a customer of the features and benefits of a product or service, and to persuade her to make the purchase. While the techniques that are used to inform and persuade others are extensively developed in professional salespeople, these are essential life skills that everyone can make use of.

LIFE IS SALES

We all have knowledge, a product or a service that we offer to others and, in many cases, attempt to persuade others to acquire. Some real-life examples include:

· A job interview
· A marriage proposal
· A friendly smile to another driver, asking to be allowed into his traffic lane

We all make sales pitches every day, and often many times a day:

· 'If you do your homework, you can go out to play football.'
· 'I think you'd prefer this movie. The star is gorgeous!'
· 'Can you be here by ten? I need to leave by eleven.'

AN ESSENTIAL LIFE SKILL

Many professions, including actors and doctors, use the principles of persuasion and sales in their professional lives. But everyone can benefit from understanding the sales process and how things are sold.

sale: an exchange of goods or services, typically for money

- Consumers can make better buying decisions by understanding the approaches that sellers use
- Career professionals can use basic sales techniques to advance in their chosen fields
- Parents can use simplified sales methods to help children accept household rules

what you learn about selling can be applied throughout your life both professionally and personally

QUICK FIX: THE KEY TO SUCCESS

In our transactional dealings with others, compromise is so often the key to our success. To compromise is not to 'give in' but to share, to help others to reach their goals as they help you reach yours. To compromise is to find the common ground on which two parties can agree and to respect the areas in which agreement cannot be reached. No one gets his own way for very long, and uncompromising positions lead to gridlock, where nothing will get done.

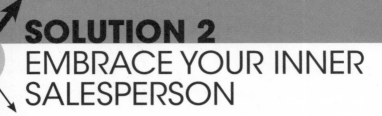

SOLUTION 2
EMBRACE YOUR INNER SALESPERSON

There are many different aspects to selling so you need to spend some time making sure you find the right sales job for you, one that fits your personality, your skill set, your needs, and your goals for the future.

use your own experience and interests to start out in a career in sales

There are no born salespeople – just people who adapt to selling easier than others. However, with a sincere desire to serve and the patience to find the job that fits best, just about anyone can succeed as a salesperson.

WHERE TO START

While many technical, retail and telephone salespeople don't have formal training in sales before accepting a job, many sales careers begin in areas of prior training or personal interest. For example:

- Computer programmers can sell software programs
- Well-travelled people can sell travel services
- Banking and financial employees can sell financial services
- Health care professionals can sell medical supplies, pharmaceuticals, health insurance, or other health-related products
- Graduates with economic or business degrees can sell financial products or services
- Construction trades people can sell property, building materials, tools and equipment, or related services
- Car mechanics can sell tools, parts or auto repair services

B2C OR B2B?

The majority of salespeople represent products and services to consumers. This is called business-to-consumer selling, which is often abbreviated as B2C. Selling to other businesses is called business-to-business selling or B2B. Here are a few things to consider when deciding which type of selling is right for you:

· Salespeople are consumers themselves, so B2C selling can be easier than B2B, particularly for newcomers to selling
· The income derived from B2C sales may be lower than B2B sales as the price of consumer items is generally less
· Many B2B sales jobs involve a specialized product knowledge for which some previous technical training is required
· With B2B selling the sale often occurs at the buyer's location rather than the seller's so it may be necessary to travel

QUICK FIX: UNDERSTANDING PAY

The financial rewards on offer are not always straightforward so make sure you are clear what the deal is:

Base salary Guaranteed take home pay

Bonus An incentive payment, awarded when an individual or team achieves predetermined financial objectives

Commission A share of the revenue on making a sale typically expressed as a percentage of the selling price

Performance-based pay The practice of paying incentives based on achieving predetermined levels of performance

SOLUTION 3
KNOW WHAT MAKES A GOOD SALESPERSON

There are proven characteristics and techniques for selling products and services. Take the time to develop these if you want to stand the best chance of being successful in your sales career.

THE KEY CHARACTERISTICS OF THE EFFECTIVE SALESPERSON

Product knowledge The more knowledgeable you are, the more able you will be to answer your customer's questions.

Knowledge of competitive products Be prepared to answer how the products you have to offer measure up against those of your direct competitors.

Knowledge of product features and benefits Help the buyer to understand your product's features and benefits, and how they beat the competition.

Communication skills Get your message across effectively – make sure your body language supports what you are saying.

Listening skills Focus not on what you have to say, but what your customer is telling you.

Persuasion skills Hone techniques to guide people to make the decisions you want them to.

Professional skills Foundation skills, such as building contacts and good record keeping, should not be neglected.

QUICK FIX: BELIEVE YOUR OWN PITCH
The very best salespeople have an unerring conviction in themselves, their profession, their product or service, their colleagues and their company. If you're trying to convince people that what you have to offer is the best thing for them, you must first convince yourself.

what is sold and to whom will dictate the most appropriate selling technique

THE KEY SELLING TECHNIQUES

Sell on features and benefits
Buyers don't purchase products and services – they actually buy features and benefits; you need to help your customers to understand how the features relate to benefits they need or want. See Solution 48.

Sell against the competition
Your product or service doesn't have to be the best in the world; it only has to meet the buyer's requirements better than your competitors do. See Solution 11.

Sell on value Rather than selling on price, you will be far more successful if you sell on value. See Solution 47.

Use the soft sell Use suggestion and gentle persuasion to make a sale rather than aggressive pressure. See Solution 4.

Friendly selling Help customers to make informed decisions but don't overstep the mark. See Solution 49.

Sell on reputation Trust is key to productive transactions. See Solution 57.

Sell problem-solutions Help buyers to solve specific problems. See Solution 35.

Practise consultative selling
Help buyers make informed decisions. See Solution 36.

SOLUTION 4
THE GOLDEN RULE OF SALES

'Never impose on others what you would not choose for yourself.'
Confucius

Golden Rule: Selling applying what you know as a buyer to becoming a better seller

The Golden Rule of Sales advocates that you should sell to others as you would like them to sell to you. Golden Rule Selling isn't necessarily easy, but then isn't that true of any selling? However, with Golden Rule Selling you will discover how you can often reach your own goals by helping others reach theirs.

WHAT DO YOU WANT AS A BUYER?

To understand what the Golden Rule of Sales actually entails, this question must be answered. As a typical consumer, you will want purchasing transactions to involve:

- Trust
- Honesty
- Helpful attitude
- Acknowledgment as an individual
- Listening to your needs
- Accurate information
- Options
- Clear explanations

And you will also want the salesperson to honestly answer your unstated question, 'Should I buy it?' – to assist you in making your decision and to be your guide in the buying process rather than pulling or pushing you through it.

'However you want others to treat you, treat them likewise.' So says the Golden Rule, a universal law advocated by all of the major religions and belief systems around the world including Hinduism, Buddhism, Confucianism, Jainism, Judaism, Christianity, Islam and Baha'i. It is also known as the Ethic of Reciprocity and it is a fundamental moral principle. Imagine how the world would change for the better if all lived by the Golden Rule.

the rewards of Golden Rule Selling are greater than those of Do-Whatever-It-Takes Selling

QUICK FIX: GOLDEN RULE DON'TS

- Don't use high-pressure sales tactics on buyers
- Don't attempt to put yourself on a higher status than the buyer
- Don't condescend or be rude to the buyer
- Don't pretend that you know everything there is to know
- Don't use intimidation to coerce buyers
- Don't ask personal questions unless invited

BENEFITS OF GOLDEN RULE SELLING

Selling as you want to be sold to is a nice philosophy, but does it work? It's altruistic, but is it practical? Buyers may yearn for an honest, trustworthy, helpful buying guide who can assist them in making informed decisions, but can you build a satisfying sales career on it? Definitely, yes. In fact, your career can thrive as you develop resources that many other salespeople don't have, such as loyal customers, referral business and buyer's trust.

SOLUTION 5
UNDERSTAND THE DECISION-MAKING PROCESS

When customers make a decision to purchase a product or service, they generally follow the same process: need, choice and commitment. Your job is to help your buyers to define their need, consider the best choices, and make a commitment.

a decision is the process that leads to a selection from among variables

DECISIONS, DECISIONS, DECISIONS

Each day is filled with hundreds or thousands of decisions, most of them small and inconsequential with the odd life changing one thrown in:

- 'Should I go to work today?'
- 'Which way should I drive to work today?'
- 'Should I buy snack before going into the office?'
- 'Where will I have lunch?'
- 'Should I ask for a raise?'
- 'Should I leave a little early?'
- 'Should I apply for that new job?'

BREAKING IT DOWN

Let's take as an example the decision to stop for a snack before going to the office.

Identification of a need You decide that a cake is just what you need.

Criteria You want a pastry rather than a sponge cake, but you don't want to travel out of your way.

Research You consider the cake shops on your route.

Analysis The Co-operative supermarket has a range of French pastries.

Choice You arrive at the Co-op. More decisions!

BE READY TO HELP WHEN HELP IS REQUIRED

While buying a boat or a car is a much more complex decision than buying a pastry, the actual process is similar. Identify the need, develop the decision criteria, do the research, analyze the research, and make choices. With complex decisions, such as buying a boat, there will be dozens of choices involving a variety of criteria – finances, dock location, number of passengers, typical use, speed requirements, and so on – and that's when the guidance that a salesperson can offer is invaluable.

How often have you visited a home superstore, only to find that you are on your own when making a selection or finding a product? Is it really possible that all the shop assistants can be on their break at the same time leaving customers to fend for themselves? It is for this very reason that many customers often prefer to shop in independent retail stores, where help is so much easier to get when it is needed.

some customers are more comfortable making decisions on their own, while others will be looking for help

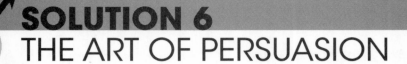

SOLUTION 6
THE ART OF PERSUASION

Whether you are an estate agent, a sales assistant, or a rather nervous suitor, persuasion can help you get your message across and accepted by another to successfully conclude a transaction.

You can persuade others by appealing to their reason or their emotions, or both. Whatever type of customer you serve and whichever type of sales job you have, the art of appropriate persuasion will be one of your greatest sales tools.

THE REASONED APPEAL

When buying a product or service, purchasers want to know what it is, how it works, and what benefits they will derive from it. They want to know the facts. Depending on what you are selling – a simple product, a complex service, or a concept – you can appeal to others by using various types of reasoning to convince them of the validity of your facts as the following examples illustrate:

Logic 'You want something that will clean stubborn stains on enamel – XYZ has been proven in scientific tests to clean enamel easier and better than any other stain cleaner.'

Rhetoric 'XYZ is the best stain fighter available.'

Proof 'Let's test XYZ on this stubborn stain.'

THE EMOTIONAL APPEAL

Salespeople and other persuaders often use emotional appeals to help make a sale. Should they? That depends on what is being sold. Selling property, for example, involves the buyer's reasoning of course, but if this is to be a family home, it is appropriate to use emotional appeals to help to sell – 'Imagine living in the nicest home on the street.' (This may not be an appropriate tactic, however, for selling industrial control valves.)

Many consumers consider an appeal to their emotions as a major factor in their decision to buy. However, a growing number of informed consumers expect salespeople to only use emotional appeals when they are appropriate to the product or service, and they may refrain from purchasing if the appeal is inappropriate.

If you want to find out more about the art of persuasion, there are many classic textbooks available including *Persuasion: Messages, Receivers, and Contexts* by William Rogers. Online, visit Changing Minds (*www.changingminds. org*), a resource explaining in layperson's terms how people think, believe, feel and act. It includes hundreds of articles with explanations and examples.

SOLUTION 7
HELP THE BUYER TO MAKE GOOD CHOICES

With the growth of the Internet people can buy even financial stock or cars without any help or advice from knowledgeable salespeople. They may save money, but they don't always make the best decisions, because they don't have a professional and ethical advisor to help them with the purchase.

it often seems like it's hard to find good help

This decline in assistive selling can work to your benefit. As a seller, you can focus on helping your customers to make good buying decisions. With expanded product knowledge, an understanding of features and benefits, and good communication skills, you can stand out as a helpful salesperson.

THE BENEFITS OF ASSISTIVE SELLING

The extra effort to offer genuine service to customers can help your sales career in many ways:

- It will show your employers that you are willing to work a little harder to help customers
- It will help you to build relationships with customers who trust you
- It will earn you repeat and referral customers – the source of future sales
- It will earn you more sales and more commission
- Higher sales can help your career progression

BUILDING TRUST

your job is to initiate and build mutual trust with your customers

To override the stigma often attached to the selling profession (see Solution 10), some salespeople refer to themselves as 'associates' or 'buyer consultants'. But a title won't convince people to trust you.

- Trust is built by not giving people a reason to disbelieve you
- Trust is offering personal information and expecting others not to abuse it
- Trust is believing that what someone tells you is true
- Trust is acting upon the knowledge of others
- Trust is an invaluable asset in any transaction

In this world of nearly 7 billion people, it's nice to be acknowledged as an individual. In some sales situations, names may not be exchanged, but you can acknowledge the individual buyer by looking her in the eye and being friendly. If names are given, they should be remembered and used appropriately. As the dynamic sales psychologist Dale Carnegie said: 'Our name is, to us, the sweetest word in the English language.' Remember a person's name, and you will be remembered.

SOLUTION 8
THE POWER OF THE SOFT SELL

Everyone has had experience of a pushy salesperson – someone who will say or do anything to make a sale, who nags and bullies you into making a purchase. It is not a pleasant experience and certainly not one you would care to repeat.

In complete contrast, the soft sell – the use of subtle suggestion and gentle persuasion – depends on building a trusting relationship with the buyer. Once that bond is established, the customer is more likely to return to make further purchases.

GUIDING THE CUSTOMER

Soft selling says, 'Here are some things you should consider in making a decision.' No coercion is exerted – you simply state a relevant fact and give the buyer room to make their decision based on the information you have provided, in response to their needs and wants. The soft-sell salesperson might be heard to say:

· 'Is this feature one that you are looking for in this product?'
· 'We've sold a number of these in the last week.'
· 'I bought one for myself and I'm very happy with it.'
· 'Consumer reports recently rated these highly.'

> **the soft sell:** a subtle approach that persuades the buyer without being forceful

THE HARD SELL

Hard selling says, 'I've made the decision for you; accept it.' It is an aggressive sales technique that relies on fear and intimidation to push buyers to a predetermined decision. In some cases psychological pressure may even be exerted to generate a quick sale. The hard-sell salesperson might be heard to say:

- 'If you don't buy this today, it will be gone tomorrow and you'll have lost it.'
- 'Don't tell me that you can't afford it; I know you can.'
- 'I absolutely guarantee that you will be 100 per cent satisfied with this product.'
- 'You don't have to ask your wife; you can make the decision right now.'
- 'If I don't sell you this, they're going to fire me. You don't want that, do you?'

hard-sell salespeople are easy to spot and just as easy to walk away from

QUICK FIX: SOFT-SELL WINNING

Psychology studies show that:
- Soft sell wins more sales than hard sell
- Customers sold by soft-sell techniques are happier with their buying decisions
- Purchasers prefer to buy from salespeople who use soft selling

SOLUTION 9
SELLING – THE NOBLE PROFESSION

There is a common misconception that salespeople will do anything to make a sale. While a few reinforce this stereotype, the majority are ethical individuals who offer a genuine service to their customers.

You choose the company you work for, the products you represent, the facts you present to customers, and the persuasion techniques you use. By living by the Golden Rule of Selling (Solution 3), you can proudly say that you are 'in sales'.

THE HONEST SALESPERSON

Honesty is adherence to the facts. It is knowing as much as possible about the product or service that you sell – and not making things up if you don't know. In short, it's how you want to be sold to.

Too many salespeople feel that if they answer all questions honestly, they will lose a sale, so they make up an answer they believe the buyer will accept. The right answer is always the honest answer, even if it is 'I don't know, but I can try to find out.' Buyers can easily spot a made-up answer, and if you fake it you will lose their trust.

Golden Rule Selling can clean the tarnish from the title of salesperson

For many, the character of Willy Loman in Arthur
Miller's play *Death of a Salesman* is the classic
stereotype. Willy made a good living for 40 years
by setting aside his principles, but he gets his
comeuppance in the end and dies without money,
friends or prestige, with only a few relatives showing up
at his funeral.

THE BUYER OR ME

You get into a sale and realize that if you don't pull this one off, you
won't get your monthly bonus. All it would take is a nudge from you
for the buyer to make the purchase. Should you?

Hundreds of other decisions have led you to where you must
make this decision: the buyer or me. Use what you've learned about
the decision process: identify the need, develop the criteria, do the
research, make the analysis, and make the choice in advance.
Consistency pays off in the long run. You can make a living and still
consider what the customer wants first.

*always act with the customer's best
interests in mind*

QUICK FIX: TRUST IN TRUST

Trust is an assured reliance on the character, ability, strength, or
truth of someone or something. Once you build a reputation for
trustworthy selling, your job will be significantly easier.

SOLUTION 10
ABOVE ALL THINGS, ENJOY WHAT YOU DO

If you are starting a job in sales, you may be beginning a lifelong career – the first in a progression of jobs that will enable you to achieve your personal and financial goals. You owe it to yourself to find the most appropriate position that fits your personality, style and interests.

don't fall for the job ads that promise unrealistic incomes in sales – if it sounds too good to be true, it probably is

THE CHALLENGE AHEAD

If you adopt Golden Rule Selling (Solution 3) as your guiding sales philosophy, there are a few challenges ahead that you will need to overcome. You need to find the products or services that you can sell honestly and effectively, and an environment in which you are comfortable selling them.

The first step is to make a comprehensive list of the products and services that you would enjoy selling. Now ask yourself:

- In what environment would you prefer to sell them?
- Do you prefer selling face-to-face or over the telephone?
- Would you enjoy finding new customers or would selling to existing users be your ideal?
- Do you like to challenge yourself daily or would less-frequent challenges be more comfortable for you?

To know what you can sell best, you must first know more about yourself. Look to your training and your interests. Consider the jobs you've previously held, the products you've bought and enjoyed, the hobbies and pastimes that have given you pleasure. It is so much easier to sell things that you are passionate about.

SALES SATISFACTION

The benefits of a sales career include a more flexible workday, an income that has the potential to grow to reflect your success, and the satisfaction of knowing that you are helping others. Here are some ways to feel satisfied about the job you do:

You are a problem solver When you meet with a customer, your job is to help that person identify and solve a specific problem – do so by understanding the steps of problem solving as well as by guiding the buyer in making intelligent decisions.

You make dreams come true You have the opportunity on a daily basis to guide people in the realization of their dreams.

You can sleep well at night By selling to others as you would like to be sold to you can rest well at the end of each day.

SUMMARY: PART ONE THE PRINCIPLES OF SELLING

01   **What is selling?** What you learn about selling can be applied throughout your life both professionally and personally.

02   **Embrace your inner salesperson** There are no born salespeople and, while some people adapt to selling easier than others, anyone can succeed as a salesperson.

03   **Know what makes a good salesperson** Recognize and develop proven characteristics and techniques for selling products and services.

04   **The golden rule of sales** Sell to others as you would like to be sold to.

05   **Understand the decision-making process** Help customers to define their need, consider the best choices, and make a commitment.

06   **The art of persuasion** The skill of guiding buyers towards making a decision by appealing to their reason or their emotions, or both, is one that you must learn and perfect.

07   **Help the buyer to make good choices** Stand out as a helpful salesperson and give your customer the assistance they need.

08   **The power of the soft sell** Use suggestion and gentle persuasion to help your buyers make decisions.

09   **Selling – the noble profession** Be honest, ethical and trustworthy, offer a genuine service to your customers, and be proud to say that you are 'in sales'.

10   **Above all things, enjoy what you do** For the first step on a long and fulfilling sales career, find the most appropriate position that fits your personality, style and interests.

NOTES

part
two

part two

IT'S ALL IN THE PREPARATION

11	Know your competition	038
12	Reconnect with yesterday's customers	040
13	Find tomorrow's customers	042
14	Connect with customers online	044
15	Find out what your buyer wants	046
16	Be sure of your facts	048
17	Don't neglect the paperwork	050
18	Know your career goals	052
19	Make a plan to succeed	054
20	Prioritize your time	056

SOLUTION 11
KNOW YOUR COMPETITION

Your competition is any business that can potentially serve your buyer. How can you compete against these businesses? By keeping up to date on exactly who they are and what they have to offer. In this way you can give yourself the competitive advantage by making sure that what you have to offer is better.

You need to get on their mailing lists and do online research – even ask your customers who they buy from when they don't buy from you. To be a smarter seller, you need to think like a buyer.

BEATING THE COMPETITION

Most products are a standardized commodity. The tube of toothpaste bought from one store is exactly the same as that available at dozens of other stores nearby. A retailer can have a competitive advantage over other suppliers either by offering lower prices or by providing greater benefits and service that justify higher prices. For example, they might:

· Provide better service with friendly, considerate cashiers always ready to offer a helping hand
· Make shopping more convenient by staying open longer hours
· Offer discounts on toothbrushes with each tube of toothpaste bought

FIND OUT MORE

Put your buyer hat on and check out your competition. The only way to beat them is to find out as much as you can about their selling strategies:

- Search the Internet to identify who your primary competitors are, i.e. those who sell the same things you do to your customers
- If they have a website, visit it frequently checking prices, service and other factors that draw buyers in
- Sign up to receive their email newsletter

competitive advantage: an advantage over competitors gained by offering greater value

your product doesn't have to be the best, it just has to be better than your competitors

A bear was chasing two men. One man took off his shoes and threw them away. The other said, 'Taking off your shoes won't help you outrun that bear!' The shoeless man responded, 'I don't have to outrun the bear. I only have to outrun you!' Sometimes a little extra effort can put you at the front of the pack, so make sure you do what you need to outrun your competition.

SOLUTION 12
RECONNECT WITH YESTERDAY'S CUSTOMERS

Tomorrow's sales depend on finding customers today. So how do you go about locating qualified buyers for what you sell, or 'prospects' as they are often called. The rules of engagement are similar, whether you are selling consumer commodities, business products, or industrial services – and a very good place to start is with yesterday's purchasers.

WINNING THEM BACK

You may have prospective buyers waiting to order from you, and they are your company's previous customers. So why aren't they buying from your company right now? The reasons could include:

- Their sales contact left your company
- Your competitors made them a better offer
- Their business changed
- They simply forgot about your company's services

If they bought from your company once, they could be in the market to do so again. Prioritize your efforts to:

- Identify previous customers who have not ordered within the last year
- Update the existing contact information
- Make a call to identify the reason(s) why they are no longer buying from you

YOUR CHANCES OF SUCCESS

prospect: a potential buyer or customer for your products and/or services

When contacting previous customers, remember you are not the problem, but you may offer the solution. A great opener is:

'I've just joined our company and wondered if you can help me. I see that you used to purchase from us, but now you don't. Can you tell me why so that I can do a better job in the future?'

In many cases, you'll find that prospects only need a reminder, a short sales message, to start thinking

by listening to your customer you have a chance to re-establish a relationship

about your company again. If there was a problem that caused the communication break down – a poorly delivered order or a personality clash with the previous sales-person – by listening to their side of things you have a chance to re-establish a relationship. Even if you are unable to resolve the problem, your efforts may at least open the buyer's mind to consider your company again.

QUICK FIX: ASK FOR HELP
One of the quickest ways to disarm a prospect, customer, supplier or colleague is to ask for their help. If asked sincerely, most people will take a moment to help another. 'Help me' is a powerful technique for diffusing situations in both your business and personal life, but don't overuse it.

SOLUTION 13
FIND TOMORROW'S CUSTOMERS

Prospective buyers are all around you. In fact, every one you know or meet is a prospective buyer of something, but who is a prospective buyer for what you sell? The answer is not always straightforward. It can entail geographic and economic factors, it can depend on the time of year or the status of your employer's inventory, and it more often than not involves research on your behalf.

LOOK TO THE COMPETITION

Your competitors' customers are valuable prospects. Firstly, if they are buying from your competitors, they are potential buyers for what you are selling. Secondly, if your products or services can better satisfy their needs, they should be your customers. You need to identify why your competitors have won their business and determine how you can win them over to your company. Of course, the final decision of who to buy from is up to the buyer, but you owe it to yourself and the customer to offer that choice.

prospecting: the process of searching for and finding qualified customers for your product or service

treat competitors' customers as your prospects

FUTURE BUYERS

target market:
customers deemed most viable for your product or service

If you identify your target market, it's easier to recognize future prospects. For example, if you are selling display units to retail clothing stores, future prospects will include those who are remodelling, opening, or thinking of buying an existing clothing store.

Find out those who can help you to find future buyers. If, for example, you want to know what retail stores are coming to your area, make contact with the shopping centre management team, the local chamber of commerce, or any other gatekeepers you can think of. Developing a relationship of mutual assistance and trust can pay off in identifying potential customers. For more on this see Solution 25. The Internet is also a great way to find future buyers, see Solution 14.

QUICK FIX: GET THE FACTS

A good free source of data is the Office for National Statistics (*www. statistics.gov.uk*). It includes current and historic data on people and households, business, industry and geography. It should be the first place you look for population numbers. In addition, you can analyze the makeup of that population by a selection of criteria including age, race, economics, and other factors.

SOLUTION 14
CONNECT WITH CUSTOMERS ONLINE

The Internet is a meeting place. People with common interests discuss their passions and pet hates via web logs (better known as blogs) in user groups and other online communities. These are potential sources of new customers for today's savvy salesperson.

the Internet is an amazing tool that can improve your sales opportunities

FINDING COMMUNITIES

How can you find communities that have an interest in what you have to offer? Here are a couple of ideas for sourcing prospects:

Google Groups Users can find discussion groups related to particular interests and participate in threaded conversations, either through a web interface or by email. Some groups are moderated, meaning someone manages the group to ensure that it doesn't collect off-topic and spam messages. Visit *www.groups.google.com*

Google Blogs This is another good way to access groups of people who are interested in a particular topic that might relate to the product or service you have to sell. Visit *www.blogsearch.google.com*

QUICK FIX: NETWORKING

Online communities are a great way to share your professional experiences. You can meet people with common interests, exchange email addresses, and develop Internet relationships. You may find friendly competitors or salespeople who don't compete in your territory that can help you keep up on the latest in your industry as well share insights about the career of selling.

KNOWLEDGE IS POWER

The Internet is the largest source of data available. You can learn to mine that data and build your knowledge towards improved sales by using information retrieval systems, called search engines, that have read and indexed just about everything on the Internet.

These search engines know where to look for data by keywords. By refining the keywords you use, you can narrow your search to get the information you need more quickly. The primary search engines include:

· Google *(www.google.com)*
· Yahoo! Search *(search.yahoo.com)*
· Live Search, formerly MSN Search *(search.live.com)*

The search engines offer guidance. Take a look at *www.google.com/help/basics.html* or *help.yahoo. com/l/us/yahoo/search/basics* for an introduction and tips for effectively using search engines, including how to use keywords and phrases to get specific results.

QUICK FIX: KEEPING CURRENT

If you want to be notified whenever your search term comes up on the Internet or in the news, join a free service such as Google Alerts. This will scan the net for your keywords and send you an email notice when discovered. You can then get real-time, daily or weekly reports on those topics. To keep your email inbox manageable, focus your keywords – your competitors' names for example.

SOLUTION 15
FIND OUT WHAT YOUR BUYER WANTS

Some salespeople believe that offering buyers too many choices can ruin a sale. Your job, as a responsible and helpful seller, is to make sure that the buyer is offered the most appropriate choices. You must ask appropriate questions to narrow down the options, then present products or services that fit your buyer's agreed-upon needs.

IDENTIFY THE CUSTOMER NEED

With experience you will be able to make a good guess at your customer's current needs, but not until they make a purchase or ask you a question will you know for sure.

To understand a customer's needs you must treat each as an individual. Listen to what he has to say, read how he says it, relate to what he is telling you, and then respond appropriately. Apply these four easy steps and you won't go far wrong.

How can you quickly determine what type of person you are dealing with and how that person prefers to be helped in the buying process? The Meyers-Briggs Type Indicator (MBTI) is a method of identifying and communicating the personalities of individuals. Personality types are coded based on attitudes (extroversion, introversion); functions (sensing, intuition, thinking, feeling); and lifestyles (judging, perceiving). MBTI can help salespeople understand themselves, their prospective buyers, and how best to inter-relate with them. More information is available online at *www.myersbriggs.org*.

ANTICIPATING PROSPECT NEEDS

Products and services are designed and marketed to solve specific problems that an identified group of buyers has. Reviewing a list of product features and benefits can help you to analyze who your potential prospects are. For example, if what you are selling is displays designed to increase traffic into a retail-clothing store, then your prospects, obviously, are clothing retailers.

The benefits list may continue with specifics that can help you focus your prospect definition even more.

PRODUCT FEATURE	BUYER TRAIT
Displays are easily moved to entryways.	The prospective store is either on a street or in a shopping centre that allows and has security for large outside displays.
Display components can be changed to fit a variety of clothing merchandise.	The prospective store offers a variety of clothing and prefers to rotate what the rack holds.
Displays include signage racks.	The prospective store wants to draw attention to the displays.

QUICK FIX: ASK YOUR BUYERS

Don't depend just on your own perceptions of what buyers want. Ask prospective buyers how they make their buying decisions. What do they consider? What do they want from the seller? How could their current sales source be improved?

SOLUTION 16
BE SURE OF YOUR FACTS

When selling products or services to your buyers it is important to be accurate in the information you provide. Buyers want to base purchasing decisions on accurate facts, and if they discover that something has been portrayed inaccurately to them, they are unlikely to return to do business with you again.

if your customer doesn't believe what you say, your sales message is lost

BUILDING BELIEF AND TRUST

Trust is reliance on the honesty and character of another and it is vital to a transaction. As a buyer, you wouldn't buy from someone you didn't trust. So how can you build trust in your prospect's mind? If you are courteous and friendly from your first contact onward, most prospects will offer you the opportunity to develop trust. Build on that opportunity by:

· Being accurate in all statements you make
· Being respectful of your prospect's opinion or queries
· Having the key facts at your fingertips so you don't waste the prospect's time
· Offering supporting information, such as studies or reports that confirm what you have said

If the buyer accepts that you can back up what you say, the thought of 'Is this true?' will not occur. The buyer will believe you and you are closer to making the sale.

QUICK FIX: OWNING UP

Errors arise from honest mistakes: the list of product specifications weren't carefully reviewed before publication; a misleading statement may have inadvertently been made; the purchaser may have misunderstood an accurate statement. Mistakes happen. The task of a responsible seller is to immediately correct an error as soon as it is identified. Doing so can actually enhance your image as a knowledgeable seller in a buyer's eyes. But don't let it happen again.

Many new salespeople quickly become frustrated because they try to sell too far outside of their comfort zone. It can be rewarding to expand your current skills, but going too far beyond them can be exasperating. For example, if you have no experience with selling to multiple buying groups, develop the required skills before you attempt to do so. Consider, is there someone in the company you work for who you can apprentice yourself to so that you can develop the skills you need to be successful?

SOLUTION 17
DON'T NEGLECT THE PAPERWORK

Salespeople have to do a lot of paperwork – there are orders to take, forms to fill out, prospect records to update and file. To ensure your future success, you must identify and use essential sales records.

IDENTIFYING THE ESSENTIALS

Keep records of the products or services you offer, the prospects and customers to whom you sell, and the profits you make from doing so.

Product records This is key data about what you sell. Product or service data sheets (sometimes called sales sheets) often include most of the relevant facts, but you may want to record additional information to help you persuade prospects to buy.

Prospect records Information about prospects and customers, sometimes known as a customer profile. This might include such information as the name of all decision-makers in a company, as well as the date and results of all contact made with them.

Profit records A record of what you have sold and what commission was earned. Some of this is automatically calculated by employers and reported to the sales staff, but keep your own records to ensure that errors don't cost you income.

THE PERILS OF SLOPPY SALES RECORDS

customer profile: a document outlining critical information about a particular customer

Let's consider a few situations that could occur if you don't keep adequate sales records, none of which is good for business:

· Customer orders don't get processed quickly or at all
· Customers receive the wrong or insufficient merchandise
· You lose valuable customer contact information
· You call buyers by the wrong name
· You forget to call back a customer when promised
· You don't receive commissions on products or services you've sold
· You miss opportunities for referral business
· Your employer doesn't recognize and reward your efforts

keeping track of sales and commissions will help you to prioritize what and how you sell in the future

QUICK FIX: CONTACT DATABASE

Historically, many salespeople used business cards as their contact database. Business card wallets were a collection point for the numerous business cards that salespeople received daily. As these cards are too small for making many notes, electronic customer databases became preferable. In the past these had to be updated manually. Today, lightweight and portable business card scanners are available that can scan, read and export data into most contact-management software programs. They plug in to a port on your computer and are well worth the small investment required.

SOLUTION 18
KNOW YOUR CAREER GOALS

Salespeople are goal-orientated people: goals will be set for the number of prospects found, the number of customers served and the number of sales made, and to be successful they must keep track of how they are doing against those goals.

Setting goals can provide you with a guiding force to help you to achieve what you want in your career.

SET EFFECTIVE GOALS

Goals must be:

· Specific
· Measurable
· Time-targeted
· Realistic

'Earn £50,000 in sales commissions this year' is a good example of a goal that is specific, measurable and set in time. However, is it realistic? If this is your first year in sales – and £25,000 in commissions is a more realistic first-year revenue target – setting a goal of £50,000 will only discourage and frustrate you. A more effective goal might be 'Increase my sales by 10 per cent each month'.

If you are new on the job and you are not sure what your sales goals should be, ask your manager. He will know what everyone on the team is selling and what to expect from new employees. Follow his guidance until you can establish your own goals.

PRIORITIZING GOALS

Some goals will be long-term goals (to be achieved in 3–5 years), some will be short-term (to be achieved in a year or less), while some will be related to a specific project. To make sure that you are always working on the most important goals, you must prioritize them.

You will often find that there will be conflicts due to lack of time. For example, you may have identified 14 business and personal activities for Tuesday, but you know you can't get to them all, so you follow a list of tasks in order of importance. In the same way prioritize your career goals by determining their relative value to you.

QUICK FIX: KEEPING GOALS

Here are a few quick tips for keeping on track with your long-term goals on a daily basis:

Write them down Make a list by order of priority.

Break them down Beneath each goal write out your specific plans for achieving it step by step.

Refer to them often Post your goals as your computer screen saver or as the front page in your daily planning book.

Set weekly targets Make working towards your goals part of your everyday routine. For example, 'To develop 50 new prospects this year' breaks down into the bite-size goal 'Develop one new prospect this week'.

SOLUTION 19
MAKE A PLAN TO SUCCEED

Your success as a salesperson is based upon dozens and even hundreds of small successes.

Once you have set your goals, you must make your plans for how they can be achieved, and take the necessary actions on a regular basis to do so.

goals are just desires until they are acted upon

MAKING A PLAN

Goals are your 'career' destinations, and the plans you make for achieving them are the roads leading you there. Plans are specific actions towards your stated goals. They identify the speed and direction of your travel, the stops along the way, and your estimated time of arrival. They also note the vehicle you will be travelling in and the fuel you will need to buy – or in other words the resources you will need to be successful.

For example, if your sales goal is to help more buyers this year, first identify how many buyers you served last year. If it is 100 and your goal is to serve 20 per cent more, then your new number is 120 buyers. The plan to achieve this goal might be to:

· Spend an extra hour in the office each day

- Hire an assistant to help with the office paperwork so you can meet more prospects
- Establish a monthly goal of serving a minimum of ten buyers
- Work harder to increase existing customer referrals

Motivational speaker Anthony Robbins (www.anthonyrobbins.com) says, 'A real decision is measured by the fact that you've taken a new action. If there is no action, you haven't truly decided.' Action is the foundation to success. If you want success, you must act on your decisions.

THE HABITS OF SUCCESS

A habit is behaviour that is regularly repeated, and habits can help you to achieve your plans more efficiently. Say, for example, you decide to work an extra hour in the office each day. This will require some changes to your current behaviour. You may have to adjust the setting on your alarm clock so you can get to work earlier. Or you may decide to cut back your lunch hour or spend less time with routine tasks so you can spend more time on productive work.

But just as important as the habitual tasks of your day are the habitual characteristics you bring to your work, which include:

Commitment When you commit to a goal, you make a pledge to take action and to make it happen.

Tenacity Believe in your goals and work around or through problems until the desired results are achieved.

Flexibility Make a plan, but be ready to monitor it if and when circumstances change or opportunities present themselves, making adjustments as necessary to ensure success.

SOLUTION 20
PRIORITIZE YOUR TIME

Learning how to prioritize your time and efforts can dramatically increase your efficiency and your income. Many professional salespeople will tell you that learning to prioritize is one of your most essential skills, yet it can be difficult to know what to turn to first when there is so much to be done.

SETTING PRIORITIES

Too often, we gravitate towards the tasks that we enjoy the most or feel most comfortable doing, rather than what should be done first to achieve a desired outcome. Carry on like this in sales and you will be changing career very soon.

To determine what order to place your priorities in, you will need to review your job description and your sales goals. However, for most sellers, the following order of importance is most likely:

1 Make sure that current customers are satisfied with your services.

2 Close current sales.

3 Help buyers who are nearing a decision.

4 Start new buyers in the purchasing process.

5 Find prospective buyers.

6 Learn more about what you sell so you can better answer buying questions.

7 Keep adequate records.

APPLYING PRIORITIES

Once you've determined the order of your sales priorities, it becomes easier to work them. A good starting point is to allocate a certain amount of time to each priority every day – you will need to be flexible however because selling, as life, isn't always predictable. Some days, you may spend an entire day helping a primary customer resolve an issue; other days, you may decide that none of your current customers are sufficiently near closing, so you focus on starting a new buyer in the purchasing process (Priority 4) or even finding prospective buyers (Priority 5).

priority:
something that gets prior attention over other things

QUICK FIX: COORDINATED SCHEDULES

If support staff is in charge of setting up your schedule and there is more than one source for scheduling, make sure that it is coordinated. You don't want to go to an appointment only to discover that it has been cancelled or moved to another location. Many scheduling software programs can help you to match up schedules from various sources while minimizing conflict, so take the time to set up the coordination system, as it will be a real timesaver in the long run. As these systems are often adjusted overnight, do make sure you start each day by checking for scheduling changes so that you are prepared for the day's events.

SUMMARY: PART TWO
IT'S ALL IN THE
PREPARATION

11   **Know your competition** Give yourself a competitive advantage by making sure that what you have to offer is better than your competitors.

12   **Reconnect with yesterday's customers** Tomorrow's sales depend on finding customers today and a very good place to start is with yesterday's purchasers.

13   **Find tomorrow's customers** Prospective buyers are all around you and your success depends on finding those interested in what you have to sell.

14   **Connect with customers online** The Internet is a meeting place of like-minded people and user groups and other online communities offer potential sources of new customers.

15   **Find out what your buyer wants** Too much choice can scupper a sale – find out what your buyer needs, then offer only the most appropriate choices to address those needs.

16   **Be sure of your facts** If buyers discover that something has been portrayed inaccurately to them, they are unlikely to return to do business with you again.

17   **Don't neglect the paperwork** Keep records of the products or services you offer, the prospects and customers to whom you sell, and the profits you make from doing so.

18   **Know your career goals** The setting of goals will provide you with a guiding force to help you to achieve what you want in your career.

19   **Make a plan to succeed** Once you have set your goals, make plans for how they can be achieved, and take the necessary actions on a regular basis to achieve them.

20   **Prioritize your time** Learning how to prioritize your efforts can dramatically increase your efficiency and your income.

NOTES

part
three

part
three

GETTING A FOOT
IN THE DOOR

21	Following up on sales leads	064
22	Buying sales leads	066
23	Turning suspects into prospects	068
24	Know what you want to achieve	069
25	Make an opportunity to sell	070
26	Getting past the gatekeeper	072
27	Introducing who you are	074
28	When to make contact	076
29	Be persistent, but don't be a pest	078
30	Learn from your failures	079

SOLUTION 21
FOLLOWING UP ON SALES LEADS

Developing new sales prospects is an important priority, no matter what you are selling. Your future sales depend on finding and developing prospective buyers, so it is important to allocate some of your time to prospecting.

the more prequalified leads you can follow up on, the better your chance of a sale

Sales leads may surface from a response to advertisements, referrals from your network, and from buying contact lists (see Solution 22).

THE BEST TYPE OF LEAD
There are two types of sales lead:

Non-qualified leads Names and basic contact information for people and companies who might buy from you.

Prequalified leads Meet defined criteria related to their ability and authority to buy what you sell.

QUICK FIX: TRADING OFF CUSTOMER SATISFACTION
Your best prospects are those that have been referred to you by current customers. Whenever a customer expresses satisfaction, ask them if they have an associate who might appreciate your services, and always follow up on these while they are current. If possible, ask referrers to let the prospects know that you will be contacting them; your prospecting call will have more credibility as you are being recommended by someone they know and trust.

ADVERTISING LEADS

Many companies use magazine advertisements to elicit a response from readers – a token gift may be offered to get the reader to make an enquiry with their contact information. Sometimes, questionnaires are used to help identify and qualify enquirers. Know what the primary qualification questions are for what you sell. Examples could be, 'Do you have a computer network that is more than three years old?', or, 'Are you considering buying a new car in the next month?' Knowing the best qualifying questions can help you to identify which prospects are the most likely to purchase from you.

prequalification can assist the seller in determining the value of the prospect

It used to be that most enquiry leads came from magazine advertising, especially in industry publications where the readers already have an identified need. Adverts would include reader service numbers that could be checked off on a postage paid card at the back of the magazine. Readers supplied contact information in return for product information or reports, with enquiries being reported back to the appropriate advertisers. Today, more enquiries are being developed through Internet websites. The process is automated so that requested information is immediately delivered to the enquirer using auto-response software.

SOLUTION 22
BUYING SALES LEADS

In addition to using prequalified advertising and Internet enquiries, contact lists can be bought or prequalifiers can be hired.

To use purchased sales leads effectively it must be determined which are investments and which are simply expenses. This requires trial and error, testing sales lead sources and comparing the outcome (sales) with the costs.

In most sales organizations, managers will purchase and test sales leads, although salespeople can help in ensuring that the results are accurately tracked.

CONTACT LISTS

Contact lists are the simplest and least expensive of purchased sales leads. In most cases, the more paid for the list, the greater the prequalifying level. They typically include information such as: name, title, company, address, type of business (SIC code), annual turnover, and other data.

Many contact lists are built from existing – and not always up-to-date – databases. People change jobs or responsibilities and lists that are more than six months old can already be out of date in some industries. When purchasing contact lists, it is important to ask how recently the data has been verified and updated.

The United Kingdom Standard Industrial Classification of Economic Activities (SIC) is used to classify businesses by the type of economic activity in which they are engaged. This information can be used to produce more accurately targeted lists of relevant companies. For more see *www.statistics.gov.uk*

SALES LEAD SERVICES

the aim is to identify prospects within a pool of suspects

Sales lead services contact the suspect and ask qualifying questions (either generic or industry specific) to determine who is in the market to buy what you have to sell in the short-term future. The prequalifying may be done by direct mail, telephone, or the Internet. Qualifying questions seek to answer:

· What is their area of purchasing responsibility?
· What are their current and future purchasing needs?
· How and why do they buy?

Accurate answers to these questions can help salespeople more efficiently identify prospects within a pool of suspects. The cost of this value-added service is higher than that of contact lists. It can, of course, be undertaken in-house, and it often makes sense to do so where products and services are focused on a niche market. The advantage of in-house prequalification is that the qualifying questions can be tailored to the exact needs of the sales staff.

Direct marketing is a business function that can help salespeople qualify sales leads. Contact list names are mailed product information and asked to indicate their needs and their authority in purchasing. Those who respond are, to some extent, prequalified and can be passed on to a salesperson for further contact and qualifying.

SOLUTION 23
TURNING SUSPECTS INTO PROSPECTS

In selling, a suspect is a prospective prospect. It is an individual or an organization with the potential to be interested in buying from you in the future. Finding suspects for what you sell is relatively easy; your challenge is to qualify them for need and interest to focus your selling efforts.

suspect:
a prospect that has not been qualified yet

NARROWING DOWN THE LIST

If you are selling pneumatic nailers at wholesale, your suspects will include all building material retailers and contractors in your sales territory. That's probably a long list. Your job, then, is to narrow down the list of suspects into prospects by qualifying them. In this situation, you can broadly qualify your suspects by determining:

· If they buy pneumatic nailers
· If they buy the type of nailers you can offer – for example, if yours are designed for factory use, they won't be appropriate for retailers who sell to consumers
· If they have purchased your type of nailers in the past

For more on using business databases and sales lead services to help you to separate prospects from suspects, see Solution 22.

a school is not a suspect for wine merchants, but a nightclub is

SOLUTION 24
KNOW WHAT YOU WANT TO ACHIEVE

Before making contact with a prospect, decide on what type of sales call you are looking for. Must you meet the person face-to-face or will a telephone appointment suffice? Generally face-to-face appointments are best – it is more difficult for most buyers to say 'No' to someone who is right there.

Once you have secured the all-important meeting make it very clear about what you want to achieve at it so that both you and the buyer can be prepared.

> **call:**
> a visit or meeting with a customer or prospect

PINNING DOWN THE APPOINTMENT

Define the meeting goals Do you plan to introduce your full product line to a new buyer, or are you aiming to solve a specific customer problem?

Determine the best place to meet Generally the buyer's office; but, if the buyer has technical questions, you may prefer to meet at a location where the products can be shown and questions answered.

Be specific about date and time Always work from the buyer's schedule. Specify how long the meeting will take and keep to it.

QUICK FIX: FIXING A DATE
Offer choices that assume a 'Yes', then work towards specifics:
- 'Is this week better or is next week?'
- 'Do you prefer meeting on Tuesday or Wednesday?'
- 'Is morning or afternoon better for you?'
- 'Does 1pm sound okay, or would you like to meet later in the afternoon?'

SOLUTION 25
MAKE AN OPPORTUNITY TO SELL

Finding prospects is a vital step in the sales process. Once found, the next step is to learn how you can help solve their problems, to make an appointment to meet them in person or by phone to analyze their needs. This can be one of your most difficult challenges.

professional sellers agree that the toughest job in sales is getting time with a buyer

THE TOUGHEST JOB IN SALES

Getting time with a retail buyer typically means making yourself available to help. However, as the price of things sold goes up, so do the barriers that buyers erect. If they make decisions on major purchases for their company, salespeople inundate them with requests for their time and attention. In this situation, many buyers defend themselves with, 'We're not buying right now.'

This can be frustrating, especially for salespeople like you who sincerely believe that the solutions you offer could really help the buyer – if only you could just get some time with them. Don't give up. Do:

· Focus your message
· Develop buyer trust
· Be patient yet persistent (see Solution 29)

general benefit statement:
a pitch made at the beginning of a sales call to highlight the value or benefit that may occur as a result of your visit

QUICK FIX: DEVELOPING TRUST

How can you build a level of trust in a prospect that you barely know? The quickest way is to trade off associated trust. Try hard for a recommendation from a friend or trusted business associate of the buyer: 'Mike Simpson, your golfing partner, just bought a set of our new clubs from me and suggested that you might like to know about how they improved his game.'

FOCUS YOUR MESSAGE

The products or services you represent may be designed to solve a number of generic problems, but the buyer will only be interested in how they solve his particular problems. Your initial message must:

Benefit the buyer You will have many unique selling points in your sales tool kit –use only those appropriate to the buyer's specific needs.

Be clear and accurate Offer specifics to prove to the buyer that you may have the solution he is looking for.

Be attention grabbing Stating a primary benefit can gain a buyer's notice – most popular, most profitable, lower premiums, reduce inventory, high satisfaction, etc.

SOLUTION 26
GETTING PAST THE GATEKEEPER

Buyers with authority more often than not have a gatekeeper – a person whose job it is to keep salespeople from wasting their time.

The gatekeeper might be the general receptionist, a sales assistant, the department or buyer's secretary, or even a manager. Generally, they have no buying authority, but if their job is to screen salespeople, you must convince them about the validity of your product or service before you get the chance to convince their boss.

THE GATEKEEPER'S JOB

The gatekeeper's responsibility is not to keep you out, but to make sure that you have something of value to offer the boss. The gatekeeper will not let you pass until you are identified as someone who is valuable to the company. If the gatekeeper judges that you meet the entry criteria, you're in.

So what are the entry criteria? You probably won't know for certain, but you can make an educated guess. If the buyer you want to see is responsible for buying all office supplies for the company, then the criteria is likely to be that all salespeople must first prove to the gatekeeper that they can provide better product, better service, or lower prices than current suppliers.

gatekeeper:
the person who controls access to someone or something

SELLING TO THE GATEKEEPER

Gatekeepers may have even less time to hear sales pitches than the buyer – and less interest too. You must tailor your pitch accordingly. In most cases, your initial contact with the gatekeeper will be by telephone, so review your telephone technique (see Solution 40).

Decide on the key criteria and communicate it succinctly. Here are examples that may work for you:

- 'I only need 15 minutes of your boss's time to show your company how to reduce inventory while increasing profits.'
- 'I recently sold an automation device to your main competitor that cut their production costs by 15 per cent and I'd like to show it to your boss.'
- 'Can I send you a copy of our catalogue and call you back in a week to see if your boss is interested in meeting?'

QUICK FIX: APPRECIATE THE GATEKEEPER

Once you are in, building a positive relationship with the gatekeeper will serve you well when making future appointments. Take an interest in who he is and what he does – look for photos and mementos on his office desk to start a conversation. Always remember to say thank you, perhaps even giving a useful gift with your company name on it – coffee cups, key chains, coasters, for office staff; for warehouse or factory workers, a warm hat or jacket in the right size.

SOLUTION 27
INTRODUCING WHO YOU ARE

If you get the chance to speak directly with a buyer, be ready to impress her sufficiently to earn a sales appointment. Your plan should be to introduce yourself, appreciate the call, state its purpose, ask for the appointment, and conclude with a thank you for her time. A prepared and efficient approach will be sure to impress.

the buyer wants to know who you are, who you represent and why she should care

FIRST STEP, INTRODUCE YOURSELF
Your call has just interrupted the buyer in the middle of something else. Make sure her attention is fully focused on you before getting on to specifics: 'Ms Jones? My name is Pete . . . Pete Smith . . . and I represent Best Products.' (By giving your first name twice, you make it more memorable.) If you have any referrals, state them now: 'Your engineer, Jane Brown, suggested that I give you a call today.' If asked, make sure you can respond to the question, 'How do you know Jane?'

Why should the prospect want to meet with you? It's a vital question to ask yourself before you begin talking. Even though you may not get a chance to elaborate on this during your brief phone conversation, knowing the reason can help you focus.

WHAT SHOULD YOU SAY NEXT?

Appreciate the call

Build positive momentum from the start.

if your presentation cannot be easily delivered over the phone, don't attempt it

- 'I'm certain that you're busy, so I'll get to the point.'
- 'Thank you for taking my call. I appreciate getting a couple minutes of your time.'

State the call's purpose

The buyer is waiting to hear, 'What's in it for me?' Have your call's purpose written down in advance – reading it aloud will ensure your message is clear. Make it as individual as you can.

- 'I'm calling because I learned your company is expanding into China and I want to make sure that you know of our international business services.'

Ask for the appointment

If the prospect encourages you to offer your sales presentation on the telephone, but you are not absolutely confident of your ability to do so, keep pushing for the appointment.

- 'The purpose of my call today is to set up a meeting with you that can help you reduce HR costs.'
- 'Can I meet with you to show how we have improved investment returns by 20 per cent?'

Thank the buyer

A chance to confirm what has been agreed.

- 'Thanks for agreeing to meet me next Tuesday at 2pm in your office.'

SOLUTION 28
WHEN TO MAKE CONTACT

Many purchases aren't made until there is a perceived need and a requirement for action. The proactive seller must be ready and able to contact prospective buyers at any point in their cycle of need – before, during or after.

ANTICIPATING NEEDS
Before the need
Many products and services sold require delivery before the need arises. For example, a restaurant needs to buy more tomatoes before they open the last crate. The proactive seller will:

· Help the buyer to accurately estimate usage so new stock can be delivered in advance of the need
· Sell based on anticipated needs

During the need
Selling products and services at the point of need is often easiest. For example, a plumbing contractor will have no problem convincing the customer that a burst water pipe needs fixing. The proactive seller will:

· Ensure prospective buyers are aware of the product and services they have to offer so they are the first to be thought of when the need arises
· Remind prospective buyers of their existence on a regular basis

After the need
Buyers may not be happy with the product or service they have received elsewhere. For example, after an accident is reported, some insurance agents call those involved to determine if a competitor handled the claim satisfactorily. The proactive seller will:

need: a condition that requires supply or relief

- Make contact with the competitions' customers to improve what's on offer
- Contact customers before their next need occurs

SELLING THE NEED

What you sell may be best offered before, during or after the need is acknowledged. However, when prospecting, the best time to approach is before the need, in fact before the need has even been identified. Your job is to help the buyer to understand that the consequences of the unfulfilled need are greater than the cost of fulfilling it now. By offering a solution to a potential problem, you have a viable reason to help prospective buyers. For example:

- 'Ordering two cases of tomatoes now will ensure you don't run out of fresh tomatoes over your busiest weekend'
- 'Having a plumbing system check tomorrow afternoon will ensure you don't have a plumbing emergency over the winter'
- 'Signing up to our insurance policy now can guarantee that you don't have frustrating claim problems again'

Not only must you help prospects and customers identify their need, you must also help them to see the value of fulfilling it, otherwise the efforts you make to offer a solution may not be successful. The more you help intensify the need, the less work you will have to do to sell the solution.

help the buyer to see that the consequences of the unfulfilled need are greater than the cost of fulfilling it now

SOLUTION 29
BE PERSISTENT, BUT DON'T BE A PEST

Buyers aren't waiting to receive your call. It's just an annoying interruption in a much-too-busy day. Be aware of this and you are far more likely to come away with the result you seek – an appointment for that all-important sales call.

be prepared to respond to a 'no' and you may get a 'yes' or at least a 'maybe'

BE PREPARED

Always ask the buyer if he has time to discuss an appointment. Be prepared to hear answers like:

· 'We don't have any needs to buy right now'
· 'I'm too busy to discuss it today'
· 'Call me back in a couple of months'

Don't take 'No' for an answer. Keep dialogue open by being careful not to ask questions that will end the discussion, such as 'Would you ever buy from us?' Instead, make enquiries that invite a 'Yes' response, such as:

· 'Do you buy this product?'
· 'Do you have a few minutes to discuss how to save £200 on your next purchase?'

QUICK FIX: TURNING NO TO YES
Two great responses to take the power out of 'No':
· 'I know you're a busy person and I don't want to take your time without giving you something valuable for it, so can I buy you lunch?'
· 'You're probably not in the market for this product right now, but can I show you how to save 20 per cent when you are?'

SOLUTION 30
LEARN FROM YOUR FAILURES

conversion ratio:
the number of opportunities secured versus the number of opportunities pursued

Not all buyers that you contact for an appointment will make one. If you find that your conversion rate is low, you need to know what you can do to improve your chances next time.

TURNING AROUND TURNDOWNS

Don't take it personally – it isn't you who is being turned down, it's your offer to present. Consider what you can do to improve your chances of getting a sales appointment in the future. If your product or service really is valuable to buyers, you owe it to them to overcome their objection to being sold to. Here are a few post-turndown questions to ask:

- Did I clearly present my message?
- Did the gatekeeper or buyer seem rushed or unprofessional?
- Was I rushed or unprofessional?
- What reason did the buyer give for not offering an appointment?
- What can I do in the future to counter the turndown?

QUICK FIX: DON'T BE PUT OFF

If the gatekeeper or buyer tries to put you off until another time, thank them for the opportunity, then get a date and time when you can call back. Most importantly, when you do call back, remind them it was at their invitation.

SUMMARY: PART THREE GETTING A FOOT IN THE DOOR

21   **Following up on sales lead resources** Your future sales depend on finding and developing prospective buyers.

22   **Buying sales leads** To use purchased sales leads effectively determine which are investments and which are simply expenses by comparing the outcome (sales) with the costs.

23   **Turning suspects into prospects** Finding suspects for what you sell is relatively easy; to focus your selling efforts you must qualify them for need and interest in what you have to sell.

24   **Know what you want to achieve** Aim for a face-to-face appointment and outline the meeting goals so both you and the buyer can come prepared.

25   **Make an opportunity to sell** Learn how to overcome the toughest job in sales – getting a meeting with a buyer.

26   **Getting past the gatekeeper** Although the gatekeeper may have no buying authority, you need to convince him about your product or service first before you get the chance to convince his boss.

27   **Introducing who you are** Be ready to impress the buyer sufficiently to earn a sales appointment.

28   **When to make contact** The proactive seller is ready and able to contact prospective buyers at any point in the cycle of need – before, during or after.

29   **Be persistent, but don't be a pest** When trying to get an appointment for that all-important sales call, be ready to respond to a 'no' and you will be more likely to get a 'yes', or at least a 'maybe'.

30   **Learn from your failures** Find out what you can do to improve your chances of getting a sales appointment in the future.

NOTES

part
four

part
four

THE SUCCESSFUL SALE STEP BY STEP

31	Pre-call planning	086
32	Making the most of your sales kit	088
33	Get your marketing tools ready	090
34	Open the meeting with confidence	092
35	Aim to solve the buyer's problems	094
36	Let your buyer help you towards a solution	096
37	Step into your buyer's shoes	098
38	Resolving conflict	100
39	Closing the sale	102
40	The golden rules of telesales	104

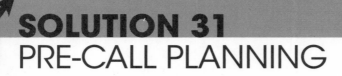

SOLUTION 31
PRE-CALL PLANNING

Once you've found prospective buyers and earned an appointment to present your pitch to them, your next task is to get ready for that all-important meeting.

Pre-call planning is essential. You've worked hard to get a foot in the door, and now you want to make the best impression you can. Preparing for a sales call can be demanding, especially the first few times you do it.

There is essential research to be done if you want to best represent your employer while offering your buyer the most appropriate solutions to their specific problems.

focus on the prospect and the problems they face, and present your product as the solution

Sportspeople often visualize their performance as a mental practise before the physical event to prepare them for action. Why not try it yourself just before making an important sales call? Relax your mind and imagine the location where you will be presenting. See yourself arriving early for the meeting with ample time to set up your presentation equipment. Now imagine sitting next to your prospect. You are comfortable as you run through your presentation, calmly answering any questions or objections raised. Presentation complete, imagine yourself writing up the prospect's order. A confidence-boosting exercise like this will help you to deliver your best efforts.

THE VITAL STEPS OF PRE-CALL PLANNING

Learn about the prospect Find out all you can about the individual buyers and the companies that they represent – who are they, what do they make or sell, how much do they sell and to whom, who owns them?

Understand the buyer's problem Do you have the information you need to clearly define the primary problem your product can solve?

Brush up on the product Know the features and benefits of the products you represent – especially those that you intend to offer as solutions at your sales call.

Tailor the presentation The sales call is not a fact finding meeting; it's an opportunity to show you understand the buyer's problem and that you have a viable solution. What do you want the buyer to think when your presentation is over? This is your goal, so now make sure the presentation you give leads to that objective.

Be prepared for objections Make sure you are ready to deal with any questions the buyer may have with a well-thought out answer.

QUICK FIX: A GOOD START

- Don't get lost – ask for directions or GPS mapping coordinates so you can find your way
- Don't be late – plan to arrive at least 15 minutes early to check out the room and prepare your presentation
- Don't keep them waiting – ask for a mobile phone number if delayed by unforeseen circumstances

SOLUTION 32
MAKING THE MOST OF YOUR SALES KIT

Salespeople use a wide variety of tools to help customers better understand the features and benefits of the products and services that they have to offer.

Your sales kit can range from a product sample to a slick PowerPoint presentation. You must build a winning tool kit appropriate to what you have to sell and who you have to sell it to.

customers need to be able to depend on what you say

KEY COMPONENTS

Whatever you sell, you must know both your products and customers very well, and you must earn your customers' trust so they will purchase from you. Your personal sales tool kit should include Knowledge, Information and Trust or KIT for short.

K is for... Knowledge of the product or service you represent – it is essential you know more about what you sell than your customer does.

I is for... Information about buyer needs – find out everything about your customers so you can help them address their problems.

T is for... Trust that must be earned – if you're confident knowledgeable and respectful your customers will trust you to assist them in their buying decisions.

PRODUCT KNOWLEDGE

Whatever you sell – razor blades, radio advertising or industrial regulators – you must know more about it than your customer does. Your employer can provide basic product knowledge, but if necessary find out more:

· Talk to the designers and engineers
· Speak with the marketing people
· Ask existing customers what they know

Find out about your competitors' products too, and again make sure you learn more about them than your customers do. Identify and understand each unique selling point that their products offer over yours.

USP: a unique selling point – a feature and its benefit to the customer

It may surprise you to learn that all USPs are not necessarily unique. Wonder Bread, a popular brand of loaf in the USA, was advertised as 'helps build strong bones twelve ways'. The bread is enriched with calcium and other minerals and vitamins – the same ones used by other major bakers. What's unique is the bakers of Wonder Bread were the first to use this feature as a primary marketing point to sell their bread.

SOLUTION 33
GET YOUR MARKETING TOOLS READY

Most products and many services sold require tangible sales tools such as samples, brochures, videos and other devices. You need to gather these tools and use them as appropriate to support your sales efforts.

Always make sure you have the most up-to-date material available, because if you don't your competitors may.

samples help buyers become more involved in the purchase

THE PRODUCT SAMPLE

For many products sold, one of the best sales tools you can have is the product itself. Even if you're selling industrial bolts by the thousands, a single bolt can help a buyer make the connection and help you to make the sale.

In some cases, a sample product isn't practical. However, always try to use something that tactilely represents what you are selling, a cutaway that shows internal components, for example; or if the primary product feature is its sturdiness, the sample can be a piece of the sturdy material that it's made from.

A drummer is a travelling salesperson that solicits orders for products using a sample and other marketing tools. The drummer's job is to solicit or 'drum up' interest in his products using a portable sales tool kit, taking orders that will be fulfilled and delivered by others.

MARKETING MATERIALS

Marketing materials support the selling of products or services.

Printed materials Includes sales brochures, signs, posters, research reports, pamphlets, product data sheets, sales scripts, business cards.

Audio/video materials Includes presentation slides, audio sales tapes, videotape and DVD presentations, web content.

Corporate merchandising Includes anything that has the company or product brand name on it such as coffee mugs, T-shirts, hats, emblem jackets, key chain fobs.

FOCUS ON THE BUYER'S NEEDS

Don't overload the buyer with unnecessary facts and figures; prune out the information to best address his needs.

Determine what the buyer knows already Find out what level of technical understanding he has and tailor your pitch accordingly.

Match the buyer's pace Don't run when offering product knowledge. For example, explaining how your new hydraulic widget works won't be helpful if you haven't first determined a basic understanding of hydraulics.

Reach the finishing line together Even if you know the perfect product to solve your buyer's problem, resist the temptation to blurt it out. Walk the buyer through the options to the best solution.

QUICK FIX: KEEPING INFORMED

Allocate at least 10 per cent of your time learning new things – details of new products, new applications for current products, what your competitors are offering, and how best to help buyers solve their problems.

SOLUTION 34
OPEN THE MEETING WITH CONFIDENCE

There is a tried-and-tested process that you can follow to get a meeting off to a confident start and it involves just four simple steps: the greeting, breaking the ice, making the transition and stating the goal.

Once you develop a relationship with a buyer, the steps may be shortened and even combined, but initially this structure ensures that you engage with the prospect so that she is ready to hear what you have to offer.

THE MEET AND GREET

The first step is greeting the prospect. Use the prospect's name first in order to gain her attention, and clearly state who you are and the company you represent:

- 'Hello, Ms Buyer,' (smile, offer hand to shake, pause), 'I'm Frank Seller with Best Products.'

The second step is to break the ice, to find some common ground so that the prospect feels at ease in your company. Your pre-call planning will have given you ideas for conversation openers, and a quick glance around the office may provide you with even more. Here are a few examples of possible icebreakers:

- 'Bill Turner suggested that I give you a call to meet you in person.'
- 'I see you're a golfer. Where do you play?'
- 'This restaurant has a great sushi bar. Have you ever had a meal here before?'

MOVING INTO THE SELL

Some prospects prefer to avoid the inevitable sales presentation and instead are happy to continue to chat. Others prefer to get on with the business in hand.

fast or slow, let the prospect set the pace

Take your cues from the prospect. As you develop sales call experience, you will better recognize when the prospect is sufficiently at ease with you to want to begin the presentation. If this is not apparent, you will need to take the initiative and transition the conversation to the selling process.

The final stage in the process is to state the goal of your meeting. This defines what you will be discussing. Once the goal is confirmed by the prospect, you can begin your sales presentation. If you discover that she sees the goal differently, it's important to identify that difference before continuing and to make any necessary adjustments before you begin).

QUICK FIX: READY TO MOVE ON

Watch and listen for a few telltale signals that indicate your prospect is ready to make the transition to selling:
· They pause and look at you expectantly
· They ask, 'What can I do for you today?' or 'What do you have for me?'
· They appear bored or impatient

SOLUTION 35
AIM TO SOLVE THE BUYER'S PROBLEMS

The majority of your prospects, buyers and customers meet with you to review your products and services in the hope of solving a problem for their employer or their customers. So learning how to identify problems and to find and sell solutions to them are valuable assets.

maintain your credibility as a problem solver to keep the buyer's attention

WHAT'S THE PROBLEM?

From your pre-call planning you probably have a good idea of what the prospect's problem is, at least in general terms – to increase profits, reduce costs, improve relationships with customers, etc. But before you can offer a solution, you need to know it explicitly, and more importantly you need to help the prospect recognize the exact nature of the problem they have.

Ask questions Develop relevant and knowledgeable questions to guide the transaction.

Listen to the response If you have prepared well, the chances are you already know the answers to the questions you pose, but listen carefully as new information may come to light.

Clarify the response Ask additional questions if clarification is necessary.

Analyze the information Summarize the relevant facts and make sure that both you and the prospect agree on them before moving forward to offer a solution.

SELLING THE SOLUTION

There may be more than one solution to the problem. You must select the most appropriate one based on your knowledge and experience, and help the

your job is to help the prospect solve the agreed-upon problem

buyer to come to the same conclusion by following these steps:

Summarize the need Restate the problem to get agreement on it before you continue.

Develop the need Explain how the problem can have far-reaching implications and may cause related problems, to prepare them to hear your recommended solution.

Offer the solution Present the features and their associated benefits (see Solution 48).

Summarize the solution Deliver your bottom line statement – the one you have been working towards since you first greeted the prospect. This is likely to be some variation on, 'Our product can increase your productivity and quickly pay for itself.'

QUICK FIX: ASKING THE RIGHT QUESTIONS

Until you've discovered the problem that your customer needs to solve and helped them to verbalize it, you don't have a solution to sell.

· Begin with open-ended questions (what, why and how) that require more information from the customer than a simple yes or no answer

· Move on to closed-ended yes/no questions to focus the buyer on specific products and benefits

SOLUTION 36
LET YOUR BUYER HELP YOU TOWARDS A SOLUTION

Smart buyers don't want salespeople making decisions for them, but most will appreciate assistance in the buying

make it your goal to help the buyer to make a good purchase

process. Many seek collaboration – to work jointly – with the seller who knows more than they do about the product or service.

BE PREPARED TO LEAD

In the collaborative selling process the leader should be you – the seller. You will be the more experienced in using the product or service and you can offer solutions to specific buying problems.

Your job is to gently lead the buyer through the process that you know so well in such a way so that he feels he is in control. He should view you as an advisor and he should never feel coerced. Your objectives should be to:

Identify a common goal The buyer's goal is to make a good purchase, so your goal should be to help him do so.

Share needs and knowledge Establish the criteria the buyer uses to make a buying decision – what his needs are – and share information about the product or service you have to offer.

Reach a consensus Lead your buyer towards the purchasing decisions that will benefit him. Once agreement has been reached on the product or service that best solves the buyer's problem, all that's needed is to close the sale (see Solution 39).

QUICK FIX: MOVE TO THE CLOSE

If a consensus is reached, but the buyer seems reluctant to close the sale, often all that is needed is to summarize what was discovered in the collaboration. Remind the buyer of the common goal, what was learned during sharing, and restate the consensus. Conclude with: 'Is there anything else you need to know before making the decision?' If this doesn't do the trick, see Solution 38.

SO MANY QUESTIONS

During the sales call, not only will you have many questions for the buyer, but also they will have many for you. You should:

Listen to the question

· Be respectful – show you are fully engaged by setting aside your sales materials and making eye contact
· Understand what is being asked – ask for clarification if necessary

Recognize the question

· If this is a technical question that needs to be answered, provide the answer
· If this is a delaying tactic to put off the decision to buy, see Solution 38

Restate the question

· This reassures the prospect that you understand their question
· This gives the prospect an opportunity to revise, clarify, or withdraw the question

Answer the question

· This recognizes the prospect's interest in buying
· This validates the buyer's enquiry

Confirm the answer

· Once understood, you can move on to close the sale

SOLUTION 37
STEP INTO YOUR BUYER'S SHOES

One of the greatest assets a salesperson can have is the ability to relate to customers and prospects. If you can learn how to see the situation from their point of view, you will be better able to help them.

IMPROVE YOUR PEOPLE SKILLS

Listen Don't block out what the buyer wants to say by talking about every feature and benefit of the product. Ask him essential questions, then listen to and utilize his answers.

Read Not all communications are heard, and you can often tell more about someone's true feelings from her body language, the gestures and mannerisms by which she communicates her outlook or frame of mind.

Relate To understand what you hear and see, you need to feel what it would be like to be in your buyer's shoes. Consider how you would feel and what you would think if you were in his position.

Respond As you learn more about your buyer, the problem that needs to be solved, and how she makes buying decisions, you will be ready to help with appropriate responses. Often, the best response is another question. Carefully probing with questions can help direct the buyer toward a decision.

QUICK FIX: THE RIGHT WAY TO ASK

Start with open-ended questions to learn as much as you can about the buyer's needs and the problem that the product is intended to solve. Then move on to closed-ended questions to narrow the search and help guide the buyer toward an appropriate selection.

Examples of open-ended questions include:

· How will you be using this product?
· What experiences have you had with buying this product?
· What experiences have you had with using this product?
· What is the role of the person you are buying this product for?

Examples of closed-ended questions include:

· Do you have a budget for buying this product?
· When do you need this product?
· Which of these two products do you think will do the job for you?
· Do you prefer the red one or the blue?

The study of body language is valuable to salespeople, especially to those who offer products to reluctant buyers. One popular book on the topic is *The Definitive Book on Body Language* by Barbara and Allan Pease. It is an introduction to nonverbal communication among business and professional people, and it includes tips on how to adjust body language to assist the buyer in making appropriate decisions.

SOLUTION 38
RESOLVING CONFLICT

Conflict occurs when a buyer stops the process or takes other evasive action to stall the sale. It may be that the price of the product is outside of the buyer's budget, or that there is a difference of understanding or opinion between the buyer and the seller. Whatever the reason, you can't afford to ignore it.

Conflict is an impediment to moving forward in the sales process and should be addressed as soon as it is evident – and it's down to you to do so.

GET TO THE HEART OF THE PROBLEM

Agree the problem
As so often, the best way to find out what the problem is, is to ask questions:

- 'What questions can I answer for you today?'
- 'Are you having some difficulty deciding?'

Define the conflict
Responses from buyers can help you define the probable cause of the conflict:

- **Indecision** – 'I'm not quite sure what I'm looking for'

- **Lack of identified need** – 'I really don't want to buy anything, but I thought I'd have a look anyway'
- **Clarification of benefits** – 'I can't decide which one of these is better'

Develop a resolution
Once you identify the conflict, you can offer a resolution. You can help the buyer to make appropriate decisions, offer relevant product knowledge, or review the main benefits of your product or service.

HANDLING QUESTIONS

A question is just a request for additional information and can be a good indicator that the buyer is interested in what you have to offer. In fact some salespeople would claim that the sale doesn't begin until the prospect begins asking the relevant questions. Here are a few tips for how to handle them:

Don't patronize If you have already answered the question, don't draw attention to the fact. Summarize without saying, 'What I said before was . . .' or 'As I already mentioned . . .'

Answer seriously Never make light of the prospect's concern.

Don't argue Listen carefully, recognize the concern, restate it, answer it, and confirm the answer.

stall: to avoid making a decision so putting the sales process on hold

if the buyer voices an objection, be ready with a well-thought-out answer

QUICK FIX: ANTICIPATE OBJECTIONS

Planting responses to common objections in your presentation can diffuse the buyer's natural reluctance to make a decision. In fact, you can make the case against the objection before it even develops in the buyer's mind. For example:

- 'As you consider your purchase, you may think that our products are too expensive. Let me respond to that . . .'
- 'I sometimes hear buyers ask to know more about our company. It's a good question. We are . . .'

SOLUTION 39
CLOSING THE SALE

The selling process involves a number of planned steps that help prospects become buyers. The prospect has a problem that you can help solve. If you present the facts and develop trust, you may persuade the prospect to make the purchase. The sales close is the agreement to exchange – your product for a specified amount of money.

In the ideal sales presentation, the prospect may ask to buy without any coaxing. However, in most situations, you will need to continue guiding the buyer towards that decision.

WHEN DO YOU BEGIN TO CLOSE?

The close is considered by some to be the most vital step in the selling process. However, it really isn't more or less important than any other. Each step – from the opening to identifying the problem, from offering a solution to answering questions – is just as critical.

New salespeople often ask when they should begin closing the sale. Experienced professionals often answer, at the beginning of the sale. At every step of the sales process – from the greeting, through stating the goal, to agreeing on the problem – you will have planned so that you know where you want the prospect to be when you're done.

ASK FOR THE ORDER

The final step is to ask the buyer for his order. Working with experienced buyers, you may find that they will make the order without additional prompting. However, many others will wait until you actually ask them to complete the transaction. Following are a few ways to do so – all have the same function, which is to elicit a decision and action from the prospect:

- 'Can I write your order for the Deluxe Product?'
- 'Would you like the Deluxe Product in your factory by the end of next week?'
- 'Would you like one or two of the Deluxe models?'

- 'I can place the order today and have them on our next delivery, okay?'
- 'Are you ready to improve customer satisfaction by buying the Deluxe Product?'

the job's not complete until the paperwork's done

QUICK FIX: ORDER FORMS

Know by heart every part of the order forms you use and understand what your employer requires. This will avoid the embarrassment of having to return to a buyer to resell a purchase due to inadequate paperwork. Provide your customer with an order confirmation copy, which will include details such as:

- Who is buying
- Who is authorizing the purchase
- Where and when delivery will be made
- The specifics of the purchase
- How payment will be made

SOLUTION 40
THE GOLDEN RULES
OF TELESALES

Millions of sales are made every year without the buyer and seller being in the same location. Responsible telephone sales can help buyers, sellers and the environment. Think of all the time, money and fuel saved when you can do your selling by telephone.

While telephone selling may not always be appropriate, many goods and services can be sold this way. As a telephone salesperson, you may never meet your customer in person, so it is vital that you develop your vocal skills (see Solution 44). The buyer must have trust and confidence not only in what you say but how you say it, so always speak in a relaxed voice that sets the tone for your customer's responses.

THE INSIDE SALESPERSON

In business-to-business (B2B) selling, many firms employ two types of salespeople: outside and inside. An outside salesperson travels to the customer, while an inside salesperson helps the customer by telephone, sending out required information by email or post. Sometimes, they are one and the same with a salesperson spending a couple of days travelling and the rest of the week working in the office.

Once a relationship is developed with the customer, inside sales can be more efficient in terms of time and cost. Customers will appreciate your call because it helps them make or save money with little effort on their part.

THE SIX PRINCIPLES OF TELEPHONE SELLING

- Don't call unless you have a compelling reason to do so
- Be friendly, but get to the point quickly so you don't waste the customer's time
- Ask the buyer, 'Is this a good time to talk to you?' – if the answer is 'No', ask for a better time to call
- Confirm any agreements at the end of the conversation and send a follow-up note or email too
- Verify contact information – direct and mobile phone numbers, email address, postal address, working hours, best time to call
- Always speak clearly, sincerely, confidently and politely

telesales:
sales made over the phone

there is nothing more annoying than unsolicited telephone calls from persistent salespeople

Automated calls with recorded sales messages are a frustration for anyone who receives them on a regular basis. Unsolicited calls from 'real' salespeople are little better. But there is a way for people to protect themselves against telemarketing. The Telephone Preference Service (TPS) is a central opt out register whereby individuals can register for free their wish not to receive unsolicited sales and marketing telephone calls. It is a legal requirement that companies do not make calls to numbers registered on the TPS. Once a number has been registered it will become effective in 28 days, and over 1.5 million telephone numbers have been noted so far. For more details see *www.tpsonline.org.uk*

SUMMARY: PART FOUR THE SUCCESSFUL SALE STEP BY STEP

31   **Pre-call planning** There is essential research to be done if you want to best represent your products while offering buyers the most appropriate solutions to their specific problems.

32   **Making the most of your sales kit** Use a wide variety of tools to help customers better understand the features and benefits of the products and services that you have to offer.

33   **Get your marketing tools ready** Always make sure you have the most up-to-date selling materials available, because if you don't your competitors may.

34   **Open the meeting with confidence** Follow the four simple steps: the greeting, breaking the ice, making the transition and stating the goal.

35   **Aim to solve the buyer's problems** Learn how to identify problems and to find and sell solutions to them if you want to keep the buyer's attention.

36 Let your buyer help you towards a solution Smart buyers don't want salespeople making decisions for them, but most will appreciate your assistance in the buying process, so collaborate with them to find the answer to their needs.

37 Step into your buyer's shoes One of the greatest assets you can have is the ability to empathize with your customer and to see a situation from the prospect's point of view.

38 Resolving conflict It is an impediment to moving forward in the sales process and should be addressed as soon as it is evident.

39 Closing the sale In the ideal sales presentation, the prospect may ask to buy without any coaxing; in most selling situations, however, you will need to continue guiding the buyer towards that decision.

40 The golden rules of telesales If you don't have the chance to meet your customers in person, it is important to develop your telephone selling skills to ensure their trust and confidence.

NOTES

part
five

part
five

THE ART OF PRESENTATION

41	Fail to plan, plan to fail	112
42	Structuring a winning presentation	114
43	Perfecting your presentation style	116
44	It's the way that you say it	118
45	Making yourself clear	120
46	Winning them over	122
47	Sell on value, not on price	124
48	Sell features and benefits	126
49	Always be a friendly seller	128
50	Using the Internet to sell	129

SOLUTION 41
FAIL TO PLAN, PLAN TO FAIL

All sales jobs require some type of presentation of the product or service. The bigger the sale, the more information and specifics buyers need to make an informed decision. Sometimes, it may be necessary to impart this information to several buyers, and the seller will be called upon to give a 'presentation'.

Before making a sales presentation, you need to determine the objectives – what you want to accomplish – and the presentation tools that you will need to help you achieve your aims.

PRESENTATION OBJECTIVES

It is important that your presentation has no more than three primary goals. What they should be will depend on the complexity of the offering and the level of understanding among the people you are presenting it to. Know your audience – determine what they know now and what they need to know to make an informed decision. Identify the primary decision makers and ask for their suggestions before presenting to the whole group.

Three primary goals for a sales presentation for administrators on a new health plan might be:

Goal 1 Summarize the current health plan, noting its limits.

Goal 2 Explain the features and benefits of the proposed health plan, including costs.

Goal 3 Get an agreement that the new plan is more cost-effective than the old one.

AUDIENCE REQUIREMENTS

What does your audience need to help them understand the points you will be making? At the least, a clear map of what is being presented, such as a simple agenda or outline. In addition, many benefit from visual summaries – charts and graphs that review or reinforce the spoken points. These can be printed handouts, product literature, projected slides, or other graphics.

sales presentation: a descriptive and persuasive account introducing the facts, features and benefits of a product or service

in many presentations, the sale is made after the presentation is done

Most business presentations today are developed using one of the many presentation software programs available such as Microsoft PowerPoint (*office.microsoft.com*) and Apple Keynote (*www.apple.com*). The programs can be installed on a laptop computer for viewing or plugged into a separate projector for larger groups. Most take the form of a prepared slide show.

QUICK FIX: MAKE IT MEMORABLE

Your sales presentation is just a moment in time for busy people who may see numerous presentations each week. To make yours stand out, leave them with something of value that will reinforce your presentation and help in their decision-making process, such as:

- Print outs of the basic presentation outline – leave plenty of white space for them to make notes
- CDs of the presentation for review at their leisure
- Supporting documents, for example articles and white papers (authoritative reports)

SOLUTION 42
STRUCTURING A WINNING PRESENTATION

In preparing any presentation, there are three simple steps to remember – tell them what you're going to tell them, tell them, and then tell them what you told them. In other words, you must structure your presentation to include an introduction, the body – or sales pitch – and the close.

Before you start, write a sentence that you want your audience to instantly recall when you have packed up and left. Use that summary to guide you as you outline and develop your presentation.

THE INTRODUCTION

The purpose is to help the audience relax and focus on the topic. You should:

· Outline your goals for the presentation
· Impart how the audience will benefit from the presentation
· Explain the structure of your presentation
· Advise if questions can be asked during the presentation or saved for a question-and-answer session at the end

QUICK FIX: KEEPING TIME
Establish a time limit for the presentation and, no matter what happens, don't exceed it. As a guide, the amount of time spent on each part for a 1-hour presentation should be:
Introduction Less than 10 per cent– about 5 minutes.
Sales pitch 80 per cent – about 50 minutes.
Close No more than 10 per cent – about 5 minutes.

THE SALES PITCH

The body of your presentation expands on the outline presented in your introduction. You will cover each point made with features and benefits. Most presenters use the problem-solution structure. Describe a problem that members of the audience face together, and then offer your product or service as the solution. Finally, clarify why your product or service is the best solution, going through each primary feature and benefit. (For more on selling features and benefits, see Solution 48.)

make sure your audience knows what's in it for them

Visuals can help you to keep your audience's attention, but take care that they do not distract from your main message. In general, plan on using one slide for every 3 to 5 minutes of the presentation, so that's 12 to 20 slides for a 1-hour presentation.

THE CLOSE

Finally summarize what you've said and why it is important to the audience. Make sure that your summary clearly includes the benefits of your solution for the audience. Once done, thank your audience for their time and help. Do not start picking up your tools and materials. Stay in position, and as each person leaves make eye contact and smile. This will ensure that any members of the audience with additional questions will feel able to approach you.

SOLUTION 43
PERFECTING YOUR PRESENTATION STYLE

How you deliver your presentation can be as important as what you say. It is not unusual to feel anxious when you are the centre of attention facing a large group of people, but there are a few communication techniques you can learn to make your presentations more effective.

GET THEIR ATTENTION

Not all audience participants will be ready to engage with your ideas so be prepared to win them over. Here are a few simple tips to help you get – and keep – their attention:

- Relax tense participants with a humorous observation as part of your introduction
- Make eye contact with each person several times during your presentation and engage them with a smile
- Build your energy level during the presentation from moderate at the start to high by the close
- Vary your voice level from softer to louder as appropriate to make your points (for more on voice control, see Solution 44)
- Direct your audience to what they should be looking at – the current slide or the presentation sheet – by looking at it yourself
- If you are standing, consider sitting when you want participants to take time to read a specific slide or document
- To keep the audience listening, don't hand out supporting documents too early – hold up each as you mention it, then place it nearby to be retrieved at the end

LEARN TO RELAX

Public speaking can be stressful, so here are a few techniques to help you control your nerves and appear calm throughout:

- Make sure that you have all your sales tools ready at least 10 minutes before you begin; have a back-up plan in case technology lets you down
- Practise your presentation in advance so you are comfortable with your message and delivery
- Take a few moments before you begin your presentation to relax your body and your mind with yoga and meditation
- Use a support – such as a podium or table – to hold your script if shaking hands are a problem
- During the presentation, take the chance when changing a slide or flipping a page, to take a deep relaxing breath, slowly let it out, then smile and continue

Many salespeople develop their public speaking skills by becoming members of Toastmasters International (*www.toastmasters.org*). It is a supportive group that offers opportunities for members to make short speeches on interesting topics for positive critiques. There are more than 220,000 members in 11,300 local clubs in 90 countries around the world. The website offers tips on overcoming the fear of public speaking and how to make effective presentations.

SOLUTION 44
IT'S THE WAY THAT YOU SAY IT

Presentations should be alive and vibrant, yet so many are delivered as if the presenter was on a life-support machine. One key way to get your message across effectively is to work on your voice control to keep your audience engaged in what you have to say.

Avoid the monotone and aim to vary your voice level from softer to louder as appropriate to the points you have to make. And always remember, a relaxed voice portrays confidence.

THE BASIC COMPONENTS OF VOICE

Pitch The tone range that the voice produces; find the pitch that allows you to speak comfortably and confidently.

Volume The loudness of your voice; adapt this so that it is appropriate to the size of the group you are speaking to.

Quality The characteristics of voice – people may be described as having a harsh, smooth, breathy, nasal or muffled voice; aim to develop a smooth vocal quality.

Rate The speed at which words are spoken – in normal conversation most people speak at a rate of about 120 words per minute; speak too fast and listeners will tune out.

Speech habits Work to soften the edges of regional accents; articulate your words well and pronounce them as commonly used.

A WELL-BALANCED VOICE

Vocal sounds are made in the nose, the mouth and the throat. A smooth voice is one that uses these three resonators in balance so that the voice sounds neither nasal nor throaty. To develop vocal balance, try this simple exercise. The sound of 'N' comes more from the nasal area, 'O' and 'W' are formed primarily in the mouth, and 'UH' is formed more in the throat.

work on your vocal skills to give your listener confidence and trust in what you have to say

Slowly repeat these sounds to help you identify their source and practise balancing them so they resonate in all three areas.

For more on vocal training consider taking a public speaking course. For example, professional speakers learn how to develop the diaphragm, a muscle below the lungs, to control air in the lungs and reduce the effort needed to talk, as well as exercises to relax their throat, mouth and lips.

QUICK FIX: FOR A TIRED VOICE

Your vocal cords are at their most relaxed in the morning after you wake up. To help relax your vocal cords any time of the day, drink hot or warm liquids, such as coffee or tea. If you find you are particularly pitchy, a slice of lemon and a teaspoonful of honey or sugar dissolved in hot water will soothe the throat.

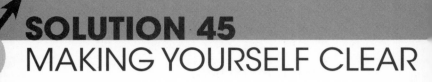

SOLUTION 45
MAKING YOURSELF CLEAR

You can have the greatest ideas in the world, but if you can't communicate them to others, you are benefitting no one except yourself.

Take the time to continually work on developing your communication skills. Focus on building your vocabulary, especially terms relevant to the products or services you sell; work on your writing skills, particularly if you are required to develop written sales proposals (see Solution 54); and perfect your public speaking skills in front of audiences both large and small. Do your research and make sure the presentations you give specifically address the needs of your audience.

vocabulary, writing and speaking skills are primary tools in a great sales career

The salesperson who talks too much has not trained himself to summarize his thoughts. This is a skill that takes practise to perfect; yet clarity of expression is essential if you want to keep your buyers on board. First and foremost, you need to know what you want to say. It's like taking a trip. If you know where you are going and the most direct path to get there, the journey is easy. However, if you don't exactly know your destination or the paths that lead there, you risk wandering around for quite a while.

KEEP IT PERSONAL

Whether you are writing your own presentation from scratch or working from a standard presentation

it is important to customize your presentation to the needs of the buyers being presented to

provided by your employer, it is important to customize it to the requirements of your buyers and to provide the solution to their specific needs. To achieve this, you must know and understand your buyers' problems, know what you are selling inside out, and know how best to present the information you have.

Work hard to keep your sales presentations fresh, current and dynamic. In addition, think like your buyer, and consider what related questions you would ask – then go and get the answers so that you are ready for any eventuality.

If you are asked questions during a presentation that you can't answer, make a note so that you are better prepared next time.

QUICK FIX: APPEAL TO THE INDIVIDUAL

Although you are making your presentation to a group, it is made up of individual decision makers. To be most effective, recognize each participant as an individual. If you know what buyers are called, use their names when answering questions. If you don't know, ask for their name – it will help you to personalize your response.

SOLUTION 46
WINNING THEM OVER

Buyers often see presenters as 'the enemy' and they may be guarded towards you. This is not unnatural – after all you are using skills of persuasion to try to get them to buy something. Hopefully, as the buying/selling relationship develops, their

when buyers are on one side of the table and the seller on the other, is it any wonder they see you as an opponent?

trust in you will build, but your most pressing job is to eliminate the atmosphere of confrontation that is common when buyers and sellers meet.

REMOVE THE BARRIERS

You want your buyers to see your product or service from your vantage point. Although you already know what problem the buyers want to solve – and more than likely the probable solution – you must be recognized as understanding their needs before they are ready to hear the solution you have to offer. They must trust that you have their best interests at heart and be assured that you can see the problem from their point of view.

If you want the buyer to come to your side of the table – to your way of thinking – first you must step over to their side.

QUICK FIX: BECOMING ONE OF THEM

Here are a few techniques that you can use for all or just portions of your presentation to reinforce that you see things from your buyer's perspective:

· Sit in the audience and control the conversation and the slides from within the group
· For presentations to individuals or small groups, sit alongside the buyers
· When presenting to larger groups, stand to one side of the audience to direct attention to the product or slides
· When presenting to smaller groups, walk around the audience

BE PREPARED TO BUILD CONFIDENCE

a well-thought-out response can turn a problem into a selling opportunity

Presentations rarely go exactly as planned and many things can go wrong from technical blips to tough questions. The time to consider these problems is before you make your presentation. If you are ready with a response for whatever is thrown at you, you will win the confidence of your audience. Ask yourself what you would do in these situations:

· A buyer begins ranting about a problem she has had with what you're selling
· A buyer gets up and walks out
· Your presentation program or computer fails
· There is a power cut
· Your demonstration model breaks

SOLUTION 47
SELL ON VALUE, NOT ON PRICE

The old business maxim is: If all else fails, sell on price. Unfortunately, too many salespeople apply this rule too quickly in the sales process. Avoid the temptation to sell primarily on price. In

> *selling on price encourages the buyer to attempt discounting future purchases from you*

the long run, you will be more successful if you aim to help the buyer understand the features and benefits of the product or service you have to offer, and how these may be better than the competition.

Help your buyer to understand the value of what you have to offer so that they are completely happy to buy from you.

SELLING AGAINST PRICE

It is not always possible to compete on price with the competition. It may be impossible for an independent retailer to compete on price with a major chain, for example, particularly if on the strength of the chain's multi-million pound budgets it is able to cut out the wholesaler and buy direct from the manufacturer – in some instances, it may even be the manufacturer!

When the exact same product is available cheaper elsewhere, your job is to point out why buying it from you has a greater value.

SELLING ON VALUE

Rather than sell on price, you will have more chance of increasing your company's profits if you sell on value. Value is worth. Your product or service may cost more, but that is because it is worth more. But be ready to back up any claims you make with facts. For example, if you were selling tyres, you might point out that:

- The cost per thousand miles driven is actually lower than cheaper tyres
- Included in the price is free repair of punctures for the life of the tyre
- The tyres you stock have the highest safety rating of all consumer tyres
- You can offer these tyres on an interest-free payment plan

value: the relative worth, utility, importance, or financial benefit that is assigned by a buyer to the product or service sold

QUICK FIX: KEEP AHEAD OF THE COMPETITION

Whatever you sell, know what your competitors charge for it. Visit their businesses as often as possible, checking prices, service and other factors that draw buyers in (and that includes the competition on the internet too). Keep thinking up new ways to attract your buyer to you.

SOLUTION 48
SELL FEATURES AND BENEFITS

If a buyer is offered a product that has features and benefits that solve a problem that they face or addresses a need that they have, at a price within their budget, a sale will be made.

FEATURES AND BENEFITS – WHAT'S THE DIFFERENCE?

A feature is a characteristic. A primary feature of a car, for example, is that it gets you from A to B. A benefit is the added value that the feature gives. The benefits of a particular car model might be that it is safe, reliable and economical, or that it makes the driver look cool and sophisticated. Your job is to point out how features relate to benefits your customers may need or want. The features and benefits list for a specific computer might be:

FEATURES	BENEFITS
22-inch flat panel monitor	Makes viewing easier without taking up much desk space
240 GB hard drive	Enables you to store thousands of digital photographs and MP3 music files
1 GB dual-channel memory	Ensures your computer operates faster and smoother
2-year warranty	An extended warranty assures the manufacturer will take care of hardware problems so you don't have to worry

POINTING OUT THE BENEFITS

salespeople sell products and services, but buyers buy features and benefits

Before you sell products, make a comprehensive list of its features and a matching list of the benefits of those features for the typical buyer. Then help individual buyers recognize the features and benefits that most apply to their needs and wants. By understanding what your products do, you can better understand who needs them.

if the features are the cooking steak, the benefits are the 'sizzle' that makes it appetizing and irresistible

QUICK FIX: FACTS BUILD TRUST

Make sure you are ready to back up the statements you make about the products you represent with succinct and understandable facts. For example: 'This article in *Consumer Digest* notes that this model has more power than any of its competitors.' Too many salespeople use unrealistic superlatives that most customers know cannot be true. Your buyers will appreciate accurate and verifiable descriptions, so think before you speak, and carefully choose your words:

X fantastic   √ most popular
X perfect   √ proven
X unbelievable   √ award winning
X best ever   √ good quality

SOLUTION 49
ALWAYS BE A FRIENDLY SELLER

Buyers want friendly sellers who will help them make informed decisions about important purchases. However, some unscrupulous salespeople will feign friendship to make a sale.

true friendship is built over time and shared experience and has no profit motive

Friendship assumes a position that you may not have earned with the buyer yet, but everyone you meet deserves friendly help. Once you have established an ongoing relationship with a buyer, know their needs and wants, and are familiar with their likes and dislikes, you may be on the road to becoming a 'good friend'.

TIPS FOR FRIENDLY SELLING

Here are a few tips to ensure you offer your customers friendly assistance:

- Ask and use the buyer's name if appropriate
- Ask the buyer relevant purchasing questions
- Listen to the buyer's responses and ask for clarifications as needed
- Help the buyer to feel that they are important to you, and worthy of your time and efforts
- Appreciate the buyer's time and efforts to purchase from you
- Be knowledgeable about the features and benefits of what you sell
- Be helpful at all times

SOLUTION 50
USING THE INTERNET TO SELL

The Internet has dramatically impacted on the sales profession – prospects can be identified and courted, products can be offered and discussed, and sales can be made without any face-to-face contact.

MAKING THE MOST OF WHAT YOU HAVE

Your employer may have a website already. Whether it is a direct marketing tool providing online sales information, or an ecommerce site through which sales can be made, make the most it:

- Study your company's website presence – put yourself in the customer's shoes and look at how it interfaces with you
- Speak with the site developer to discover its functions and features and ask the webmaster (the person or service that manages the site) about how it works
- Ask your employer for some training, if necessary train yourself by reviewing software manuals and reading books
- Get your name and contact information on the website

QUICK FIX: WEBSITE PRESENCE

If your employer does not have a website, encourage them to set one up – a simple website can cost just a couple of hundred pounds or less. In the meantime, consider promoting your sales efforts using association and network websites. For example, if your employer is a member of a trade association, you may be able to submit your email or website address for inclusion as a link.

SUMMARY: PART FIVE
THE ART OF
PRESENTATION

41   **Fail to plan, plan to fail** When giving a presentation, you must determine what you want to accomplish, and the presentation tools that you will need to help you to achieve your aims.

42   **Structuring a winning presentation** Structure your presentation to include an introduction, the body – or sales pitch – and the close.

43   **Perfecting your presentation style** How you deliver your presentation can be as important as what you have to say; learn effective communication techniques to make your presentations more memorable.

44   **It's the way that you say it** Work on your voice control to get your message across effectively and to keep your audience engaged in what you have to say.

45   **Making yourself clear** You can have the greatest ideas in the world, but if you can't communicate them to others, you are benefitting no one.

46 **Winning them over** Your most pressing job is to eliminate the atmosphere of confrontation that is common when buyers and sellers meet.

47 **Sell on value, not on price** You will be more successful if you help the buyer to understand the features and benefits of the product or service you have to offer over and above the competition.

48 **Sell features and benefits** Tell buyers what they want to know – the benefits that they will derive from the features your product offers.

49 **Always be a friendly seller** Friendship assumes a position that you may not have earned with the buyer yet, but friendly help is deserved by everyone you meet.

50 **Using the Internet to sell** You cannot afford to ignore this channel to the customer – find out what is available to you and make the most of it.

NOTES

part six

part
six

FOLLOW UP AND FOLLOW THROUGH

51	The follow up call	136
52	Keep in touch with your customers	138
53	Selling to multiple buyers	140
54	Writing winning sales proposals	142
55	Taking to the road	144
56	Work smarter not harder	146
57	Protect your reputation	148
58	Revisit your goals	150
59	Getting the job you want	152
60	Getting on in sales	154

SOLUTION 51
THE FOLLOW UP CALL

The presentation has been given, the deal has been closed, but that is not the end of the selling process – the follow up is just as important, particularly if you want to secure future sales.

Confirm the sale and make sure that the customer is satisfied with what they have bought. If there is a problem be sure to deal with it straight away, if they are happy with the purchase ask for a referral.

PICK UP THE PHONE

Call to confirm Phone the buyer to confirm the details of his order. The best time to do this is either once the order is written, or just before it is processed.

Call to verify satisfaction As soon as the order is received and in use, phone the buyer to make sure he is happy with his purchase. Does it do what you said it would; does it solve his problem?

What should you do if your buyer gets cold feet and calls you to cancel the order? Buyer's remorse is common amongst those purchasing high-price items so don't take it personally. Arguing about the sale is pointless; remain friendly and help the buyer to review the problem and solution. Summarize the sales call: review the points of agreement and resell the product or service including benefits.

THE EXIT SURVEY

Following a sales meeting or presentation, take the time to analyze how things went by using your own perceptions and by asking prospects what they

your long-term sales goal should be to develop satisfied customers

thought. You want to know what worked, what didn't, and how you can make improvements for future sales pitches. If mistakes were made, you will be able to avoid them in the future. Avoid closed-ended yes/no questions, and encourage participants to be frank with you. Find out why they decided not to buy this time, or the reason that encouraged them to make the purchase.

QUICK FIX: FUTURE BUSINESS

Lose a sale, but don't lose a customer. A sale may bring you a hundred pounds in income, but a customer, over time, can be a source of thousands of pounds in salary and commissions. If, for example, you direct a prospect to a competitive product that better addresses his problem, you may lose the sale, but the chances are that you will gain a customer who will trust you for honest, unbiased advice when they are looking to make future purchases. In addition, they are likely to refer you to their acquaintances. Always ask satisfied customers for referrals to new prospects, and be sure to ask for permission to mention their name when making contact.

SOLUTION 52
KEEP IN TOUCH WITH YOUR CUSTOMERS

Making – and keeping – contact with your customers and prospects is one of the most critical tasks in your job description. Managing customer contact systems and maintaining profit records will better place you to serve your customers, your employer, and your sales career.

MANAGING CUSTOMER CONTACT

Customer records are important. You need to know all you can about your buyers and prospects, and you need to track the history of your contacts with them. When did you last visit this customer? What were the results? Did you give them a quote? When will you hear back from them?

Just a few decades ago, salespeople recorded contact information on index cards and in a contact logbook, and finding information on contacts with a specific customer required lengthy searches through written records. Today, there are numerous customer and contact-management software programs available in the marketplace – everything from database programs to integrated network systems – that will help you to keep track of your sales performance. But these systems are only as good as the information you supply them with, and it is important to make the time to update your records on a daily basis.

the primary function of sales records is to ensure that your customers are being served as well as possible

TRACKING SALES PERFORMANCE

In sales, analysis means comparing data about one customer to others, one industry to others, one time period to others, and so on. Sales analysis can help you improve your sales performance. You may discover that hours with one type of customer are more productive than days with others, and you can correlate specific products with industries or territories where they sell better.

Factors you might want to track include sales by:

- Customer
- Industry
- Time period (daily, weekly, monthly, quarterly, annually)
- Product
- Territory or location

Efficient record keeping helps you and your employer to:

- Identify which types of customer most need your efforts
- Recognize those customers that are the most profitable to your company
- Confirm the bestselling products or services within the company and within your customer group
- Assess what time periods are most productive in selling
- Analyze the similarities among unprofitable customers
- Find and fix sales process problems

if Customer A buys more from you than Customer B, Customer A will be the higher priority

SOLUTION 53
SELLING TO MULTIPLE BUYERS

In the ideal sales scenario, the proportion is one buyer to one seller. You get to speak directly with the person who will make the final decision. However it is often the case that many people make or influence the decision to buy, so you must be able to identify, analyze and help multiple buyers in a transaction.

IDENTIFY THE DECISION MAKERS

There are two levels of authority within a decision to purchase: deciders and influencers. Deciders are those who have the ultimate authority to say 'yes' or 'no' to the purchase; there can be more than one decider for any purchase. Influencers do not have direct authority to make the purchase, but their input can affect the buyer's decision to a greater or lesser extent. You need to find out:

· Who the ultimate decision makers are
· How much authority each of these have in the final decision
· Who and what influences them in the decision-making process

QUICK FIX: DECISION-MAKERS UNKNOWN

The rule is: If in doubt, sell. That is, assume that those you are presenting to have sufficient authority to make the decision or at least to influence the decision to purchase. It is better to temporarily assume greater authority than it is to later discover that you should have been selling to someone you were ignoring.

GROUP DECISIONS

No matter how large the group of buyers that makes the purchasing decision, they are all individuals with specific needs. Treat them as such to help them make better collective decisions.

As you develop relationships with the individuals in decision groups, you'll be in a better position to determine what they need to know. Use your knowledge to build their trust: if you can get them to think of you as a non-voting member of the decision group, you can better analyze the individuals, understand the group dynamics, and how they work together to make buying decisions. From within the group, you can inform, advise and influence to keep it progressing towards a sale.

aim to get the decision group to consider and treat you as 'one of us'

QUICK FIX: MULTIPLE BUYING GROUPS

If you have to sell to separate groups or committees of buyers, you may be presenting to groups of people who have diverse interests in the transaction. If you are involved in a complex sale like this, consider each as a separate sale. Each presentation has a different goal and agenda to different decision makers and influencers. Plan accordingly.

SOLUTION 54
WRITING WINNING SALES PROPOSALS

A sales proposal is an offer to sell a product or service to solve a business problem. The more expensive the products and services you sell, and the more complex the buying decision, the more likely it is that you will need to develop a sales proposal, so it's important to know how to plan and write an effective one.

WHAT MAKES A SUCCESSFUL SALES PROPOSAL?

Whether it comes in the form of a letter or a 100-page document, its aim is always the same: to answer a buyer's questions regarding their request. Some proposals may be required to follow a standard format (if it is receiving numerous proposals, this makes it easier for the organization to compare the responses in each), but if this is not the case, your proposal should contain the following:

The requirements summary Taken from the request for information/quotation/proposal; for initiated proposals, simply summarize the perceived problem.

The details Focus on details identified by the buyer, then go on to outline how you will solve the problem and at what cost. Provide objective and comparative facts, not opinions.

The executive summary A substantive one-page summary of the main points for busy decision makers; avoid unsupported superlatives (best, world-renowned, excellent) and present just the facts.

MEET YOUR DEADLINE

As soon as your deadline is known, develop an action plan to complete the proposal in advance of it. Working from the end date back, break the project into tasks that need to happen before the proposal can be delivered. Allow sufficient time for fact checking, internal review and editing. Allow extra time for contingencies that may delay progress.

Once completed and delivered, keep a log of all sales proposals to schedule and track follow-up. Once the bid is awarded, and whether you have been successful or not, contact one of the decision makers and ask for feedback on the process. Finding out why the winning bidder was selected will help you to better prepare and win future proposals.

sales proposal: a written document to summarize and support the offer to sell to encourage the prospect to buy

QUICK FIX: PERFECT PRESENTATION

· Make sure your proposal is reviewed for technical accuracy and grammatical errors before submission
· Verify how many copies of the proposal are requested – some buyers will prefer to make and distribute their own copies from a master, while others will want you to do this
· Make sure that your proposal package is easy to read and avoid fancy bindings that can make disassembly and copying difficult
· If given the chance, deliver your written proposal to decision makers in person

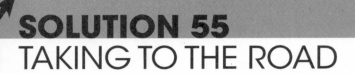

SOLUTION 55
TAKING TO THE ROAD

Some sales jobs require that you travel more than others – annually, seasonally or all of the time. If you enjoy travel and don't have family obligations, the life of a travelling salesperson can be rewarding. However, for many, working on the road is difficult.

to get the most from your trip, understand exactly what you want to achieve from it

Travel is a logistical strain with irregular accommodations, unpredictable food, and the frustrations of scheduling delays. Good planning can help you to survive – and even enjoy – sales trips.

THE SUCCESSFUL SALES TRIP

To ensure that your sales trip is a success, you must:

·   Know where you are going and why
·   Make sure you have the things you need
·   Be efficient in your work
·   Enjoy yourself

QUICK FIX: PLAN AHEAD

Make sure that you have a comprehensive list of your needs before you make the trip, especially if you will be away from replenishment sources. For example, your presentations may require equipment that you must ship ahead. Or you may need adapters for the different electrical systems in foreign countries. Or you may be required to attend a formal dinner and need appropriate attire.

ENJOY THE EXPERIENCE

It is as much your employer's responsibility to organize a productive sales trip as it is yours. Ask colleagues or managers for their advice on what to pack, what to expect, and what to do if problems arise.

- Plan your days loosely and allow time to fix unexpected problems
- Use the latest technology and communication tools to keep in touch with business on the road
- Interview your employer about business expectations as well as off-time opportunities at your destinations. Take a camera, see the sights, and shop for souvenirs; find opportunities to enjoy what you do and where you are
- Stay in contact with family and friends

QUICK FIX: INTERNET MEETINGS

Web presentation software enables you to conduct a full sales presentation in a distant office while sitting at your desk. WebEx (*www.webex.com*) is a program that manages meetings over the Internet. It's similar to a visual conference call. Using Internet cameras mounted on the computer monitor, it sends videos of participants to each other so it seems like a face-to-face meeting. In addition, presentations can be offered and participants can use their keyboards and mice to point or add to the presentation screens. Fast Internet connections are required. Many sales offices use similar products to hold staff meetings or to meet with suppliers around the world without travelling.

SOLUTION 56
WORK SMARTER, NOT HARDER

If you can harness the power of your email and voice mail to help you to sell, and run your sales call schedules more effectively, you are well on your way to maximizing your sales efforts without having to burn the candle at both ends.

EMAIL SELLING

Emails can be valuable sales tools that succinctly present your information to others with the least effort and expense.

- Respond to enquiries by sending product information in or attached to emails
- Ask current customers if you can contact them via email and at what address
- Ask website visitors to sign up for a newsletter or other sales information

You can develop standard selling and response messages in your email software's draft box, then customize and send them as needed. Make sure that the subject line clearly states something of interest to the receiver, and that the email concludes with a 'signature' giving your contact information.

email marketing is an efficient and effective way to reach customers with your sales message

Popular email systems allow an ending message, called a signature, to be automatically appended to outgoing messages. It can be customized and normally lists your position, how to contact you, and a short sales message. To decide what to include, you should ask yourself what is useful to the receiver. The signature can be a default for all your email addresses or you can have unique signatures for individual accounts.

EFFECTIVE VOICEMAIL SELLING

You appreciate the benefits of getting callback messages when you are in a sales call, on another phone, or at lunch, but when making contact with customers, you prefer to talk to them direct. This is not always possible, so learn effective voicemail selling. Prepare short scripts to help you to remember to include pertinent information. Examples include:

· 'Returning your call. Sorry I missed you. Here's how to contact me again.'
· 'Following up on your question. Please call me back for the answer you need.'
· 'We have a new product or feature that may be profitable to you. Please call me.'
· 'Calling to make sure that your product arrived safely and to answer any installation questions.'

Make your script conversational and include your contact information, including best times for them to reach you in person.

QUICK FIX: CALENDAR FEEDBACK

Feedback is output used to adjust input. You use it in a hundred ways every day as you drive, speak, eat and work, making correcting changes in the input to alter the output to a desired level. By making note of your calendar adjustments, you can schedule your time more effectively. For example, if a meeting with Customer A takes half an hour rather than the planned one-hour, when scheduling your next meeting with that customer, plan it for half an hour.

SOLUTION 57
PROTECT YOUR REPUTATION

Once you build a widely known reputation for trustworthy selling, your job will be significantly easier. If your buyers trust you to be honest and accurate, they will buy more from you. You will have worked hard to build your reputation, so you need to work equally hard to protect it.

BUILDING YOUR 'BRAND'

One of the greatest assets you can have as a seller is a reputation for honest and accurate dealings with others. It will gain you repeat and referral customers. To develop your sales reputation:

- Sell as you want to be sold to
- Only sell products and services that you can honestly represent to buyers
- Be accurate and truthful in your transactions
- Encourage appreciative buyers to tell others about their experiences with you
- Give out your business card to build name recognition

Brands are valuable. Millions of pounds are spent on developing consumer trust in a brand of cars, restaurants, toothpaste, etc. The majority of products that you sell will have brands. Your employer has an advertising and promotional budget to develop your company's reputation for selection, service, or price.

INFLUENCING HOW OTHERS THINK

Influence is the act of producing an effect without exerting apparent force. The subtlest persuaders used by salespeople include these positive actions:

· Smiling
· Making an affirmative comment
· Appreciating someone's ideas or actions
· Acting on someone's suggestion

use your power of influence to help your buyers along the process towards the best solution

Once you've earned a buyer's trust and respect, you have significant power to influence, but you should never abuse it. If the purchaser asks your opinion on the relative merits of specific products or services, make your answer appropriate to the buyer's needs rather than to your own or those of your employer. By doing so, you will be building a more trusting relationship.

QUICK FIX: DRESS FOR SUCCESS

People are sold, in part, through visual perceptions. Follow these guidelines if you want to dress to impress:

· Select understated accessories, jewellery and fragrances
· Make sure that your hair is clean, neat and professionally styled
· Be sure that your apparel is clean, neatly pressed and of the appropriate size
· Select clothing that draws attention to your face rather than your body
· Keep colours and designs simple and not distracting
· Choose apparel that is more formal than that of your typical customer

SOLUTION 58
REVISIT YOUR GOALS

As seen in Solution 18, goal setting can help you to achieve your priorities in life. However, life changes on a daily basis and some of those changes can impact your goals. Those who are able to adapt to changed circumstances have the greatest opportunities to succeed.

Priorities require adjustment based on feedback – employers and family will thrust some goals and priorities upon you, and a staff cutback at work or a medical emergency at home can shuffle your priorities in a moment. Therefore, it is important to see your goals as guidelines for planning your days – consider them as aspirations, not requirements. Be ready to adjust smaller goals to meet larger ones as situations change.

Imagine a rugby or football match where no one kept score. What's the point? What would motivate the players and the fans? How would everyone know who won? The same is true in sales. Keeping score helps you measure progress towards your goals. How you keep score depends on the specifics of the goals: prospects, customers, orders, territory, sales amount, and so on. For example, if your goal is to increase the number of new prospects you see each month, then your score card will measure prospects. If the goal is a level of income, progress will be counted in pounds.

STAYING MOTIVATED

It can be hard to keep motivated on a daily basis, but here are a few ideas to help you maintain your focus:

keep a balance between your job and your personal life

- List your reasons for selling and keep them where you can easily refer to them
- Review your referral references to reinforce how your efforts have helped others
- Recognize your successes on reaching short-term goals rather than repeatedly looking forwards to the long-term ones
- Live in the now – enjoy what you are doing today
- Reward yourself for success – make time for a fulfilling social life, and relaxing and stimulating holidays
- Turn to your career mentors for help and advice – at best, they have the experience to guide you, at worst they can offer a sympathetic ear for the problems you face

QUICK FIX: VISUALIZE SUCCESS

One motivator for helping you to keep committed to your sales goals is to visualize the results of doing so. For example, if your goal is to increase your sales income this year by 25 per cent over last year, imagine the benefits of achieving this. Picture yourself being able to take more or better holidays, providing your family with the things they want, or purchasing something you've always desired.

SOLUTION 59
GETTING THE JOB YOU WANT

Getting your dream job can be your ticket to a more rewarding life, so you need to put as much time and effort into preparing to acquire it as you would a sales pitch or presentation. Develop your CV, get ready for the interview and make sure you know what to expect when you are hired.

PREPARING YOUR CV

Your curriculum vitae (CV) helps employers understand the features and benefits of hiring you. It must clearly represent your credentials and your career goals, and should include the following:

Experience Tell employers what you've done but only include experience that is relevant to the position you are applying for.

Credentials Outline what you know or have been recognized for; use measurable terms – customers, revenue, percentages, etc.

References Communicate what others say about you; make sure you get permission to include referees first.

Contact Give contact details and list times when you are available to discuss employment.

QUICK FIX: THE FUNCTIONAL CV
Usually a CV is organized chronologically, listing your jobs and responsibilities by date, starting with the most recent first and working backwards. However, if you have moved from job to job, you may be better represented by a functional CV where you group your employment by job function rather than by employer.

THE COVERING LETTER

Focus the employer on why you are the right candidate for the job. There are four common elements:

the purpose of a CV is to earn an interview; the function of a covering letter is to get the CV read

Subject 'Thank you for considering my credentials as a sales manager for your company.'

Qualifications summary 'I offer your firm five years' of progressive experience in selling to business clients... (and elaborate).'

Focused qualifications 'Most importantly, I am a proven self-manager with experience of helping other salespeople to reach their own and their employers' goals... (and elaborate).'

Urge to action 'Please contact me at your convenience to discuss your position further and to discover how I can help your business grow.'

THE INTERVIEW

The job interview is your opportunity to sell yourself face-to-face. Prepare yourself:

- Before your interview appointment, go over the job description, and re-read your covering letter and CV
- Consider what questions the interviewer might ask based on these documents and be ready to answer them
- Be focused on your interview – don't walk in thinking about the parking ticket you might get
- Don't be late, dress for success, and be confident in the outcome
- Relax and enjoy this opportunity to sell yourself
- Prepare a few questions to discover what the employer has to offer you in terms salary, benefits and career development

SOLUTION 60
GETTING ON IN SALES

Just as the products and services that you sell require presentation, so do you. Whether you are selling yourself to your current employer (seeking a raise), a prospective employer (seeking a job), or to a new prospect (seeking a sale), you must package yourself as well as your products without bragging, boasting or embellishing facts.

HOW TO BECOME A BETTER SELF-SELLER

To know the extent and value of your skills you must evaluate yourself objectively. A good way to do this is to prepare a self-resume – this is a bit like a CV, but the difference is that the end result is for your eyes only, so you can be as thorough as you like. Include knowledge, training and experience that contribute to your selling skills. Consider the variety of your sales experiences as well as the types of products or services that you have sold. State facts in measurable terms and write them down. Think of yourself as a product and ask yourself: What are your features? What are the benefits of those features? What types of problems can your product (you) solve for others (your customers)?

one day you may sell ice to the Inuit, but until then stick to the facts

Sometimes the best way to see ourselves is through another's eyes. It can help, therefore, when seeking to understand yourself and your qualities more objectively, to ask the opinion of a friend or colleague.

BUILDING YOUR TRACK RECORD

As you grow and succeed in sales, you will gain valuable experience and meet measurable goals. To ensure you can impress future employers, follow these important steps:

Keep records Establish and maintain an effective record-keeping system to track prospects, customers and sales; it will give you the specifics you need to show progress and success in your career.

Win awards In most sales organizations, awards are frequently given to recognize success; aim to win as many as you can and proudly display the trophies too.

Get recommendations Collect recommendations from satisfied customers. Ask for a letter of recommendation on their letterhead, or if you can add them to a list of people who will be advocates for you (useful to give to prospects).

Build confidence Self-belief depends on facts rather than desires; you either have reasons to believe in your abilities or you don't. By building the evidence of your previous successes – by keeping records of your achievements, winning sales awards, and getting recommendations from your customers – you can believe in your future success.

SUMMARY: PART SIX FOLLOW UP AND FOLLOW THROUGH

51   **The follow up call**   Confirm the sale and make sure that the customer is satisfied with what they have bought; if there is a problem, be sure to deal with it straight away.

52   **Keep in touch with your customers**   By managing customer contact systems and maintaining profit records, you will be better placed to serve your customers, your employer, and your sales career.

53   **Selling to multiple buyers**   Often many people make or influence the decision to buy, so you must be able to identify, analyze and help multiple buyers in a transaction.

54   **Writing winning sales proposals**   A sales proposal is an offer to sell a product or service to solve a business problem; know how to plan and write an effective one.

55   **Taking to the road**   Good planning can help you to survive – and even enjoy – sales trips.

56   **Work smarter not harder**   Use your email and voicemail to help you to sell, and run your sales call schedules more effectively to maximize your sales efforts.

57   **Protect your reputation**   One of the greatest assets you can have as a seller is a reputation for honest and accurate dealings with others. These will gain you repeat and referral customers.

58   **Revisit your goals**   Those who are able to adapt to changed circumstances have the greatest opportunities to succeed.

59   **Getting the job you want**   Put as much time and effort into preparing for job applications as you would a sales pitch or presentation.

60   **Getting on in sales**   To advance in your career, you must learn how to sell yourself as an important product with proven services.

NOTES

INDEX

appearance 149
appointments 69–71, 74–5, 80, 86–7, 92–7, 102–3, 106–7, 145

B2B selling 15, 104
B2C selling 15
benefits 16–17, 71, 126–7, 130
body language 98–9
branding, personal 148–9
business cards 51
buyer's remorse 136

calendar feedback 147
career goals 52–5, 59, 150–1, 157
closing sales 96–7, 102–3, 107
communication skills 16, 98–9, 120, 130
competition 16–17, 38–9, 42, 58, 125
competitive advantage 38–9
compromise 13
confidence 17, 92–3, 106, 123, 155
conflict resolution 100–1, 107
consultative selling 17
contact details 51, 66, 67
conversion ratio 79
covering letters 153
curriculum vitae (CV) 152
customer profiles 50–1, 138–9, 156
customer satisfaction 64, 136

decision-making 20–1, 24–7, 29, 32–3, 55, 96–7, 107, 140–1
disarming customers 41
drummers 90

email selling 146, 157
emotional appeals 23
empathy 98–9, 107, 123
ethics 28–9, 33

exit surveys 137

failure, learning from 79, 81
features 16–17, 126–7, 130
follow ups 135–9, 156
friendly selling 17, 128, 130

gatekeepers 72–3, 81
general benefit statements 71
Golden Rule 18–19, 28, 30–2

hard sell 26–7
help, asking for 41
honesty 18–19, 28, 30, 33, 148

influence 149
inner salesperson 14–15, 32
introductions 74–5, 81, 92

job applications 152–3, 157
job satisfaction 30–1, 33

marketing tools 90–1, 106
motivation 151
multiple buyers 140–1, 156

names, using 25, 128
needs, buyer's 21, 46–7, 58, 76–7, 81, 88, 91, 95
networking 44
noes, dealing with 78–9

online sales 44–5, 58, 129, 131, 145
orders 103, 136

paperwork 50–1, 59, 138–9, 155
pay systems 15
persistence 78, 81
personal qualities 16–17, 32
personality types 46
persuasion 13, 16–17, 22–3, 26, 33
planning 86–7, 106, 112–13, 130

pre-call planning 86–7, 106
presentations 111–31
price, selling on 124, 130
prioritizing 56–7, 59
problem solving 17, 31, 70–1, 87, 94–7, 106–7
product knowledge 14, 16, 48–9, 59, 87–9, 91, 127
product records 50
promotion 154–5, 157
prospects
    locating 40–5, 58, 137–9, 156
    records 50–1, 138–9
    turning suspects into 68, 80

reputation 148–9, 157

sale process 85–107
sales analysis 139
sales kit 88–9, 106
sales leads 64–7, 80
sales opportunities 70–1, 80
sales performance tracking 139
sales proposals 142–3, 156
samples 90
scheduling 57
soft sell 17, 26–7, 33
stalling 101
summarising 97, 120
suspects 67–8, 80

target markets 43
telesales 104–5, 107
timing 21, 114
travelling 144–5, 156
trust 25, 29, 48–9, 71, 88, 127, 149

unique selling point (USP) 89

value 17, 124–5, 130
vocal quality 118–19, 130
voicemail selling 147, 157